TROLLEYS

TROLLEYS

Riding and Remembering
the Electric Interurban Railways

RUTH CAVIN

HAWTHORN BOOKS, INC.
Publishers / NEW YORK

1000

Contents

Acknowledgments   vii

Introduction   ix

 1 The Trolley Takes Off   3

 2 As Different as Houses   16

 3 An Interurban to Anywhere   44

 4 The Shortest Distance . . .   59

 5 Acts of Man, Acts of God   63

 6 Three Long Rides   84

 7 Too Good to Last   100

 8 Intensive Care   107

 9 Trolley Jollies and Juice Jacks   117

10 Riding to Scale   125

11 "Rails Alive '75"   146

12 Museums That Move   165

13 Is Anything Coming?   192

Trolley Museums and Related Attractions   201

Index   215

BROADVIEW

Acknowledgments

Invariably the many people I approached in the course of working on this book went out of their way to give me every possible kind of assistance and information—with unfailing courtesy and kindness. Rather than try to name them all here, I simply note that as they appear, undisguised, in the body of the book, it should be understood that my sincere thanks accompany their presence.

I owe a great deal to the authors of *The Electric Interurban Railways in America*,[1] George W. Hilton of Stanford University and John F. Due of the University of Illinois, who together have written what surely must be the definitive history of electric interurbans in America. I'm grateful to the compilers of *The Steam Passenger Service Directory*,[2] which surpasses its title by including almost every trolley museum as well. I found Bryant A. Long and William J. Dennis's *Mail by Rail*[3] a great help in the section on interurban rail post offices.

A number of people have searched out and taken photographs and otherwise provided illustrative material for me, often unhesitatingly loaning me irreplaceable films or prints. Photo credits are given in the captions, but I want particularly to thank Newton K. Gregg,

1. George W. Hilton and John F. Due, *The Electric Interurban Railways in America* (Stanford: Stanford University Press, 1960).
2. *The Steam Passenger Service Directory* (Middletown, N.Y.: Empire State Railway Museum, 1975).
3. Bryant A. Long and William J. Dennis, *Mail by Rail* (New York: Simmons Boardman Publishing Co., 1951).

John Sheldon, Frank W. Schlegel, Blair Foulds, G. J. Sas, and the editors of *Model Railroader* magazine. When I began looking for illustrations, I found them and many others to be unbelievably generous, not only in permitting me to use their material, but in going to endless trouble to supply it. It is hard to thank them adequately.

I am anxious to acknowledge—quite loudly—the assistance of those on whom I have leaned most heavily: Captain Herbert W. Dosey, Ron Brown, John Sheldon, Herman Rinke of the Electric Railroaders' Association, Frank Schlegel, Jr., and, most particularly, a man to whom I am quite content to be hopelessly in debt—the peerless trolley modeler, scholarly historian, and delightful source of all kinds of trolley information, Blair Foulds.

Introduction

For those of us old enough to remember getting around town in streetcars, yet young enough to take for granted superhighways and passenger jets, the notion of riding through woods and pastures in a trolley car has an element of fantasy. It belongs with the stories of capricious New York City bus drivers who suddenly take off, passengers and all, for Miami Beach; of whimsical ferryboat captains who strike out across the Atlantic with their load of Staten Island-bound commuters. But in many parts of this country, less than fifty years ago, trolley cars between towns and cities were an American commonplace—a part of what Lewis Mumford has approvingly called "a total transportation network that met different human needs at different speeds."

The electric interurban railways were an extremely short-lived phenomenon, as social phenomena go, but in the years between the turn of the century and the 1920s, they did much to bring industry to the Middle West, multiply land values, transport workers to jobs, and vice versa. The interurbans literally revolutionized the lives of farmers, and they expanded the physical and social horizons of every class, making possible country homes for the urban wealthy, college educations for the small-town well-to-do, larger territories for the traveling salesman, and cheaper and fresher milk and vegetables for those who lived in the cities. They accomplished this while operating through the countryside at a level of speed, convenience, cleanliness, and comfort that makes it clear why Mr. Mumford and his fellow social thinkers look back on the interurban trolley with something more than nostalgia.

The interurbans, which came along in the very late nineteenth century, fit into the place between city trolley cars—"mass transit"—and the steam railroads. They served this purpose for a relatively brief period because they were superseded by the automobile, which was invented at the same time but which took longer to perfect as a means of transportation available to practically anyone.

The real world seldom arranges itself into neat categories, and to try to arrive at a rigid definition of an interurban railway would be to wrench the variety of interurbans and near interurbans and part interurbans into an artificial uniformity. They can, however, be defined well enough to explain them, and to equip the reader, were he to meet one, to recognize it, even in some disguise. Professors George W. Hilton and John F. Due in their indispensable source book, *The Electric Interurban Railways in America*, describe true interurbans in this manner: "Railways that shared most or all of the four following characteristics: electric power, primary emphasis on passenger service, equipment that was heavier and faster than city street cars, and operation on streets in cities but at the sides of highways or on private rights-of-way in rural areas."

A veteran interurban enthusiast with whom I spoke told me that he considered any trolley an interurban if it ran on railroad schedules rather than on the kind of headway you find with city trolleys, buses, and rapid transit. Another listed four distinctions, elaborating a bit on Hilton and Due: "Interurban wheels were larger than those on streetcars, motors were 50 to 160 hp, as against the streetcars' 20 to 40 hp, the interurbans ran at about 45 miles an hour more than the streetcars were capable of, their ride was smoother and heavier, and the cars were furnished more comfortably—more like long-distance vehicles than like city transport."

A former railroad man, whose enthusiasm for the interurbans goes back many years, makes the sole distinction of speed. The true interurbans, he says, are the high-speed railways; anything with a running speed of over fifty miles an hour fits into the category. The heavy interurbans ran at 60 mph and faster; when the tracks were new, some could, I'm told, hit 100.

We are dealing here principally with high-speed interurbans, but if one that falls somewhat outside that definition obtrudes upon the narrative, we will not refuse to listen. (From time to time, even city streetcars will somehow sneak into this account, though we shall then be forced to cry, with the March Hare and the Mad Hatter, "No room! No room!")

A number of people associated with the electric railroads that ran out of Cleveland until 1938 are living in retirement around that city, and I have been lucky enough, in working on this account, to have met them. I have visited and talked to former interurban men—motor-men, conductors, electrical engineers. In other places I have found "railfans" and "trolley jollies," those who make models and restore old cars, collect "hardware," and preserve the history of the lines. Many of them appear in these pages, generously sharing with us their knowledge of and enthusiasm for the electric cars they love.

TROLLEYS

1
The Trolley Takes Off

In the 1890s a farmer and his family could go, on or behind a horse, to visit a neighbor or to a nearby village. Not many farmers, however, lived so close to the city that their horses could make it there and back the same day. The steam railroads served well for long trips, but they made few stops in the smaller towns and none in the countryside. The residents of Chardon, Ohio, a small community less than 30 miles east of Cleveland, used to travel 125 miles to Pittsburgh to do their shopping, because the Pennsylvania Railroad took them there. Farms in the area around Chardon supplied the city of Cleveland with produce, but in the summer vegetables and fruits arrived wilted and dusty from the long wagon ride, while in winter, when wagon roads were closed, such produce as went to market had to go by rail to the grocers of Pittsburgh. Illogical situations of this nature could be found all over the United States.

But in 1893, the first electric interurban railway in the United States began running in Oregon, and the country immediately and enthusiastically began traveling by trolley.

The interurbans were the offspring of city trolley cars, which, in turn, evolved from the horsecars. The horsecars were popularly called "hayburners," and with reason—the ratio of hungry horses to the cars they hauled was often as lopsided as eight to one. The cost of maintaining their extensive stables was high, and the animals' working lives were short and consuming; after a career of horsecar pulling, the horse had depreciated to the point where he couldn't command much of a

It started with the horse. . . . Philadelphia in the 1860s.

price for any secondary purpose. In addition, the owners lived with the permanent apprehension of another "Great Epizootic" (the equine equivalent of an epidemic), such as the one that in 1872 killed thousands of car horses.

Small steam engines and cable cars had already been tried in urban transit, and electric cars had also been attempted, without much success.

Some of the "bugs" in the earliest electric streetcars were more exasperating than discouraging. Frequently, the controls caught fire; when the firemen turned out and aimed their hoses at the conflagration, they were as often as not knocked flat upon the cobblestones by the charge of electricity that ran back at them up the stream of water.

All hands to the rescue of a derailed electric car—a frequent incident with early trolleys.

There were more serious problems, too. Often the gears would go out of alignment, breaking the connection between motor and wheels. The vibration of a heavy motor on the driving platform of what was really a flimsy horsecar was too much for the joints; the cars soon began to fall apart.

In 1888 a young former assistant of Thomas Edison's named Frank Julian Sprague, who might quite accurately be called "the inventor of the electric trolley," successfully electrified a twelve-mile streetcar line in Richmond, Virginia. He worked out a system of "wheelbarrow" suspension, in which one part of each engine was attached to the axle, keeping the gears in alignment, and the other part spring-mounted to the frame to absorb jolts. The Sprague arrangement worked so well that no sooner were his electric cars running in Richmond than orders began to pour in from all over the country. By the next year there were 200 electric streetcar lines in operation or being built, of which more than half had been equipped by Sprague and more than 90 percent were built according to his general plan or patents.

Sprague connected his cars to the power supply with overhead wires and a pole on the car roof. At the top of the pole was a small wheel that ran along the wire. This wheel, a descendant of a little four-wheeled wagon called a "troller," which connected an earlier car to the wires, was named "trolley." The word derives from the Middle English "trollen," "to roll or ramble"; this is the root, as well, of "trolling" for fish and of "trollop," a loose or slovenly woman. Other streetcar designers tried sending power into the car through the rails—they were there, they were metal, why not use them? But puddles, switches, and horses that wanted to stand with two feet on each track proved the impracticability of this seemingly logical system and, with a few exceptions, the trolley became standard for electric cars.

With street trolleys running so rewardingly, and travel between towns so difficult, the next step was inevitable. Take the trolley out to the country! But that demanded more sophisticated technology.

Sprague was to provide the electric railway with a device that proved to be one of the most important in mass transit. Known by transport people and modelers alike (both of whom still use it) as "MU," his multiple unit control makes it possible to hook up a string of self-propelled cars and operate them with a single set of controls. This was not a major development for the early interurbans, since

The Jackson and Sharp trolley car works in Wilmington, Delaware, 1872.

almost invariably they ran single cars, but later many of the large railways ran passenger trains of two or more cars, and many interurban freight trains used multiple unit cars instead of simple trailers.

City streetcars operated on 600-volt direct current; the DC motors were light and easy to carry one-to-an-axle, and the current didn't have to go very far. When suburban and early interurban lines tried to adopt this same power system, they found that as the wire was made longer, there was a severe voltage drop from the friction between trolley and wire.

It was only when they worked out a way to carry the current for long distances that true interurbans became possible. Main power stations generated high voltage alternating current. (Most of the early interurban lines generated their own power.) One such station could supply the electricity for as much as 200 miles of line. The top wire of the trolley lines carried this AC current to substations along the route, and there it was converted to the 600-volt DC necessary to run the car motors. DC was preferred, even when AC current became common for other uses, because it had better torque and allowed better speed control.

The substation's main piece of equipment was a device called a rotary converter. Because these required constant attention, the substations were attached either to an interurban station or to the homes of the men who tended them, much as a rural telephone switchboard can be found in the operator's living room.

A few lines got power from a third rail, but most trolley companies were justifiably nervous about possible danger to stray children and animals. Sprague had used third-rail electrification in early trials, and was to develop the first protected third rail for the Lehigh Valley Transit Company in Pennsylvania.

In the mountainous western states, some cars were powered up steep grades by a form of alternating current that allowed them to feed back to the line, or "regenerate," the power they subsequently created rolling down the other side. In the flat Middle West this was impossible, and the typical Midwest interurbans stuck to the AC + substation = DC arrangement. Every company owned portable substations, too: cars equipped with rotaries, which could go to the point in the track where trolley cars, gathered at a fair or ball game, made more power necessary.

Once started, the interurban boom was on! Soon there were interurban trolley lines by any definition in New England (along with a vast network of rural trolley cars), upstate New York, Maryland, Virginia, Iowa, Texas . . . but the greatest concentration of interurban railways was in the Middle West, and, after that, on the West Coast. Ohio had by far the largest trackage in the country; Indiana was next. There was no Ohio town of 10,000 or more without interurban service, and although Indiana did not have Ohio's 3,000 miles of trackage, all but three towns in that state with a population over 5,000 were served by the ubiquitous electric railways.

A multiplicity of lines met at the great Indianapolis Traction Terminal, the only interurban station in the country with a train shed. Nine tracks ran into the terminal, and the large office building attached to it housed the railways' headquarters and such related organizations as the Central Electric Railway Association.

In other midwestern states—Illinois, Michigan, Wisconsin—heavy trolleys sped through the countryside. The Middle West not only severely needed this kind of transportation; it was astonishingly well-suited for it. Ohio, Indiana, Illinois, and southern Michigan were well-endowed both with fairly prosperous farmers and with towns and small cities to which these farmers wished to travel and to send their produce. The land was flat; there were few topographical headaches for anyone wanting to build a railway. Steam road service in these states was relatively sparse.

The principal entrepreneurs in interurban building were men who had already become big operators in other utilities—street railways, telephones, and the like. Building trolley lines, taking over and consolidating other complete or partially built systems ("Conceived in equity and born in sin," said one of the partners in the Northern Ohio Traction & Light Company), they managed to make large sums of money and to serve (unfortunately, as it often turned out) as inspiration for other, smaller promoters.

The names of the men responsible for the largest, most successful Ohio interurban lines read like a law firm concocted by the Marx Brothers—Everett, Moore, Pomeroy, Mandelbaum, and Appleyard. Singly and in overlapping and interlocking combinations they controlled an interest in an important percentage of the state's 2,798 miles of track.

Fired by Everett, Moore, Pomeroy, Mandelbaum, and Appleyard's collective example, anxious to get into what then seemed the most promising business proposition in the country, scores of small promoters dreamed up interurban lines of their own, although many of these never got further than paper proposals. For every ten (at least) lines that were promoted and advanced far enough to be mentioned in *The Electric Railway Journal* before dying stillborn, one was built. At one time or another eleven companies proposed lines into Tiffin, Ohio; only one got there. Every sizable town had one or more groups of local businessmen who wanted to build an interurban line, and sometimes the citizens as a whole tried to raise money for a line as a community project. But unless the line could terminate in towns large enough to support it, as did Everett and Moore's ABC (Akron, Bedford & Cleveland), it could not be profitable or even self-supporting. Sometimes a line was built, ran, and served for a time the secondary function of providing trolley transportation to the community. The primary function of every private enterprise—generating at least a small return on investment—was another matter.

Typical of such useful failures was the Cleveland & Eastern

Traction Company, which was begun by a group of citizens who wanted good transportation into Cleveland, so that they could comfortably live in the beauty spots outside of it, such as Gates Mills and Chagrin Falls to the east. It was an almost classic example of where not to run an interurban. Almost exactly at the eastern boundary of the city of Cleveland, the land becomes very hilly. When Dr. Benjamin Spock lived in Cleveland Heights, a suburb that immediately adjoins the city on the east, he traveled a mile or so each day to his office. He said that every day he went from the foothills of the Appalachians to the Great Plains. Technically, this is so. Comparatively few people lived out in Geauga County where the line was to go; and there was an extraordinarily long stretch of street running in Cleveland before the cars reached the center of the city. The line, consolidated with another that served an area nearby, failed as early as 1904, although a section of it ran, in receivership and then reorganized, until 1925—unprofitably.

In fact, although at some periods some lines or combines showed a profit, the interurban industry was never a financially healthy one. Far from being the biggest bonanza of the century, as many investors of the time believed, the interurbans were never, overall, a paying proposition. It is astonishing only in retrospect that while investors rushed to put their money in more and more new interurban lines, Henry Ford was able to raise only $28,000 of the $200,000 he felt he needed to start the Ford Motor Company. There are the usual tales of people who, even many years after the first halcyon days of the industry, sold their Ford or Pennsylvania Railroad stock to invest in interurbans.

The eager investment was spread around thinly, however, and few interurban enterprises were notably well-funded. Often, the only way a company could finish building a line was by paying off the subcontractor (the contractor was usually the promoter himself in a different hat) with shares in the company. Many an earthmoving, tracklaying outfit found itself rather bewilderedly the part owner of an interurban railway.

In one case, this led to a famous and rather comical legal altercation involving an improbable cast, which included the shouting evangelist Billy Sunday, H. J. Heinz, founder of the Pittsburgh pickle company, and the Electrical Installation Company of Chicago. Heinz, with other businessmen (J. M. Studebaker was one) had founded the Winona

Assembly in Indiana, a religious camp where Billy Sunday and some of his lesser-known but just as noisy colleagues held forth at camp meetings designed to save the souls of those present. In order to bring the public to the camp at Winona Lakes, three miles from Warsaw, the nearest town, Heinz and his associates founded the Winona Interurban in 1902. When completed, it was sixty-eight miles long, extending from Goshen to Peru.

Both Heinz and Studebaker were strict Sabbatarians, and refused to operate the railway on Sunday. The Sabbath, however, was the one day in the week when people wanted to ride the railway—the one day worshipers, and the curious, flocked to Winona Lakes to see and hear the noted Billy Sunday and the other preachers there.

The Electrical Installation Company had been paid off with several hundred thousand dollars worth of stock in the Winona Interurban. To save the Winona from bankruptcy, they wanted to institute Sunday operation. Finding insistence useless, they took the other stockholders to court. The case was decided in their favor, whereupon the manager of the line, either from sycophancy or true conviction, resigned his position, a gesture that may, or may not, have saved him from everlasting hell fire.

By the end of the second (and final) interurban building boom in 1908, tracks radiated from large and largish cities like cracks in a plate-glass window. Most were in the Middle West, although the West Coast had considerable mileage, as did Pennsylvania, and there were lines in many parts of the West and the Southwest also. New England had hundreds of miles of the area's equivalent: city trolley lines running down the middle of roads between towns. Only the South had virtually no trolley mileage outside of the cities. If you were willing to change trains frequently, you could ride the trolleys from almost anywhere to almost anywhere. Some people did—newspaper reporters, mostly, gathering data for what became a standard feature story. These were tours de force; the real beauty of the interurbans was not that they could compete with the steam roads in long-distance travel, but that they were so flexible. However, there were many lines on which it was possible to go a respectable distance in one car, either on the track of one company or on that used jointly by two or more lines. One could make an unbroken journey, for example, between Cleveland and Detroit (165 miles), Indianapolis and Louisville (117 miles), Cincinnati and Toledo (217 miles, the longest single line of all),

Fort Wayne and Northern Indian

FAST THROUGH LIMITED TRAINS
CONVENIENT, FREQUENT LOCAL TRAINS } BETWEEN { Fort Wayne, Hu

THROUGH LIMITED TRAINS, FORT WAYNE TO INDIANAPOLIS VIA PERU C

NINETY PER CENT. OF TRAINS ON TI

MAP SHOWING ELECTRIC LINES

CONNECTIONS
See time on opposite side.

Fort Wayne

FT. WAYNE & NORTH-ERN IND. CO.
Yoder, Ossian, Bluffton, Montpelier, Hartford City, Muncie, Roanoke, Hunting-ton, Andrews, Lagro, Wa-bash, Peru, Logansport, Delphi and Lafayette, Ko-komo, Indianapolis.

OHIO ELECTRIC RY. CO.
Lima, Toledo, Springfield, Columbus, Dayton, Cincin-nati.

FT. WAYNE & NORTH-WESTERN RY.
Garrett, Augurn, Waterloo and Kendallville.

FT. WAYNE & SPRING-FIELD RY.
Decatur.

STEAM ROADS
Penna Lines, C. H. & D., N. Y., C. & St. L., L. S. & M. S., Wabash, G. R. & I.

Huntington

STEAM ROADS
Erie R. R., C. B. & C.

Wabash

ELECTRIC LINES

UNION TRACTION CO.
Marion, Alexandria, An-derson.

STEAM ROADS
Big 4.

Logansport

ELECTRIC LINES

UNION TRACTION CO.
Kokomo, Tipton, Nobles-ville and Indianapolis.

STEAM ROADS
Penna. Lines
Vandalia

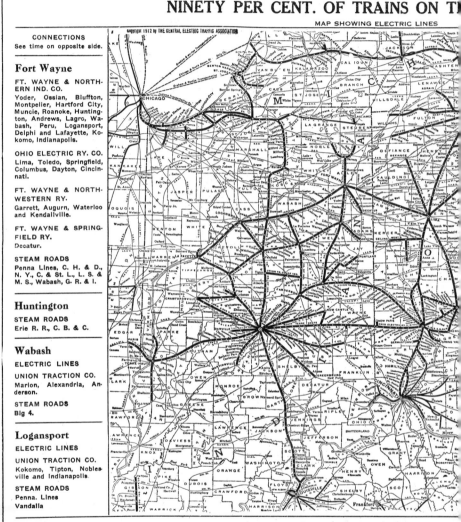

Copyright 1912 by THE CENTRAL ELECTRIC TRAFFIC ASSOCIATION

INTERURBAN FREIGHT MEANS EXPRESS SERV

Two Through Freight Trains each way a day between Fort Wayne and Lafayette. Fast Freight b
Delivery between Fort Wayne and Indianapolis. These trains make connections a

LOOK AT THE MAP AND SEE THE TERRITORY

raction Company

Wabash, Peru, Logansport, Lafayette, Bluffton,
sian, Yoder and Muncie

. SAME TIME EITHER WAY.

ST YEAR

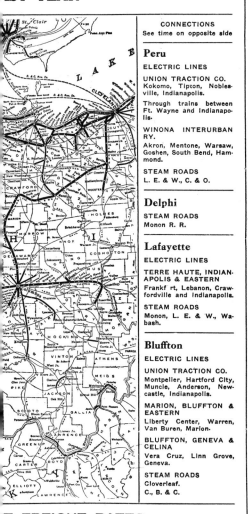

CONNECTIONS
See time on opposite side

Peru

ELECTRIC LINES

UNION TRACTION CO.
Kokomo, Tipton, Nobles-
ville, Indianapolis.

Through trains between
Ft. Wayne and Indianapo-
lis.

WINONA INTERURBAN
RY.
Akron, Mentone, Warsaw,
Goshen, South Bend, Ham-
mond.

STEAM ROADS
L. E. & W., C. & O.

Delphi

STEAM ROADS
Monon R. R.

Lafayette

ELECTRIC LINES

TERRE HAUTE, INDIAN-
APOLIS & EASTERN
Frankf rt, Lebanon, Craw-
fordville and Indianapolis.

STEAM ROADS
Monon, L. E. & W., Wa-
bash.

Bluffton

ELECTRIC LINES

UNION TRACTION CO.
Montpelier, Hartford City,
Muncie, Anderson, New-
castle, Indianapolis.

MARION, BLUFFTON &
EASTERN
Liberty Center, Warren,
Van Buren, Marion.

BLUFFTON, GENEVA &
CELINA
Vera Cruz, Linn Grove,
Geneva.

STEAM ROADS
Cloverleaf.
C., B. & C.

T FREIGHT RATES

rt Wayne, Bluffton and Muncie. Through Six-Hour
on Points for delivery to other lines.

RED BY ELECTRIC LINES

Like cracks in a plate-glass window.
Map from a Fort Wayne and Northern Indiana Traction Company timetable dated March 1916.

Indianapolis and Fort Wayne (136 miles), Rochester and Syracuse (87 miles), Buffalo and Erie (92 miles), Chicago and South Bend (90 miles, on a line that is still carrying passengers), San Francisco and Chico (183 miles), Los Angeles and San Bernardino (58 miles), San Francisco and Sacramento (93 miles), and Kansas City and St. Joseph, Missouri (79 miles). The longest trip of all without a change of cars, from Youngstown, Ohio, near Pittsburgh, to Jackson, Michigan—some 440 miles—took eighteen hours and forty-five minutes.

The longest continuous trip in a *succession* of cars was from Elkhart Lake, Wisconsin, to Oneonta, New York, a distance of 1,087 miles. You could ride from New York to Chicago *almost* entirely on trolley lines; of the 1,143 miles, 187 of them had to be negotiated by steam railroad. Mr. J. S. Moulton, an official of New York's Interborough Rapid Transit (familiarly, the IRT subway line) took the trip in 1912. Although his total traveling time was three full days and twenty-one hours, he traveled comfortably, disembarking to dine and spend the nights in hotels. The actual travel time was not the elapsed ninety-three hours, but forty-five hours and twenty-four minutes. One sixteen-hour stretch in one electric rail car covered 297 miles. The cost to Mr. Moulton was $19.67, but he confessed that he could have saved $2.00 or possibly $3.00 by buying his tickets on entering the cars.

At about that time, twenty-two businessmen from Utica, New York, went on interurban tracks to Louisville, Kentucky. Traveling by day and spending nights in hotels, the passengers found themselves being royally entertained by officials of the various interurban lines on the way. Ironically, they were traveling—on interurban tracks, it is true—in a New York Central Railroad car, which they had rented for the occasion. The great majority of interurban trips, however, were on twenty- or thirty-mile lines; many were shorter.

Steam railroads saw the new electric lines as a threat to their business, and this suspicion of the newcomers extended right down from the corporate offices to the trackmen, trainmen, and construction workers. Clashes, such as the one that took place in March, 1902, between Ohio Central Traction Company construction workers and the operating employees of the Big Four and Pennsylvania Railroads, were frequent. The Ohio Central track had been completed except for the point where it was to cross the steam road tracks at Crestline, Ohio. The interurban's franchise would expire the next day, unless the line was completely built, and the company would then lose

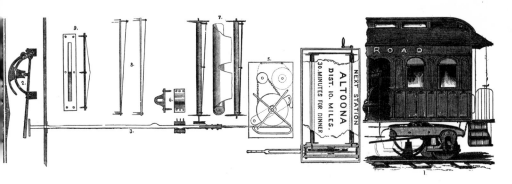

Lt. J. W. Graydon's invention to designate stations and streets on railroads and streetcars. Courtesy of the Picture Collection, The Branch Libraries, The New York Public Library.

the right-of-way. The steam men challenged the trolley men as the latter began to lay the crossing, and a fist fight began which lasted from noon until midnight! Contemporary reports don't say whether the crews brought in reinforcements or if just one group of men conducted the twelve-hour battle.

Presumably the line was laid in time, because it went into service and later became part of the Cleveland, Southwestern & Columbus Railway—one of the more than seven hundred interurban lines which have been allowed to disappear. With them vanished their well-designed private rights-of-way. It is impossible to imagine the extent to which the value of those assets has increased, and hopeless to speculate on what we could make of them now.

2
As Different as Houses

Interurban trolley cars ran often; sometimes the schedule was half-hourly and you could usually catch one anywhere in less than an hour. Although there was almost no interurban advertising, as such, the newspapers carried daily schedules. A rural rider had only to go to the nearest stop and hail the trolley when it appeared. Fares were from a half to two-thirds lower than steam road rates—about two cents a mile in the Middle West, lower in New England, and higher in the West.

There was usually no extra charge for buying a ticket on the train, from the conductor, since so few stations were elaborate enough to include ticket agents. They varied from structures built or bought especially to serve as trolley stations, through single stores outfitted with ticket windows, waiting rooms, and baggage counters, where passengers and freight were loaded on the street in front, to simply more or less arbitrarily designated points along the line, with or without small unheated shelters.

Often, every farmhouse on the route had its own interurban stop. On the midwestern trolleys, which could travel at considerable speeds on private rights-of-way, these frequent stops were a costly and time-consuming practice, and the management preferred a right-of-way that paralleled a road. But since convenience was the advantage that the interurban offered over the railroad, the trolleys were forced to stop almost at the passengers' will.

Not a very elaborate station, but it served to keep the weather off. Note the car waiting in a layby while another passes, extreme right. Courtesy of Blair Foulds.

To stop a car, most commonly a rider simply raised his arm, although a few lines had light signals. At night, a passenger wishing to hail a car took a newspaper to the trolley stop with him. When the car's headlight appeared in the distance, the would-be rider took out a match; when the car came close enough, he set the newspaper on fire and waved it at the motorman.

In towns, interurbans commonly ran on city car lines; in the country there was, in most instances, only a single track. It followed alongside of an existing road; if the road was too roundabout, or did not exist, the trolley took off across the fields.

Town franchises for street running were sometimes difficult to get; small-town merchants were apprehensive about losing trade to the metropolitan emporiums. The town governments, influenced by commercial anxieties, often made things difficult for the trolley line. In every street franchise it was stated that the interurban must pave the street between and around the tracks and keep it in repair. Some communities demanded that its members ride free within the town limits, others asked for out-of-the-question payments for the privilege of using the local streetcar track. A number of projected lines tripped on the town franchise problem and stopped there.

A Philadelphia Suburban Transit sweeper on an icy main street in West Chester, Pennsylvania, after bucking a heavy snow. Photograph by Eugene van Dusen. Courtesy of 35 Slides, Colorado Springs, Colorado.

Often an interurban car was camouflaged to look like a city streetcar, for the mollification of fussy citizens who objected to long-distance trolleys running through their streets. The car factories could also provide boxcars for interurban freight trains that were disguised as passenger cars, in case some citizen felt that the trolley line had put him on the wrong side of the track.

Most farmers gave no trouble at all over rights-of-way; indeed, they were eager to have the line. It meant not only convenient transportation, but frequently electricity as well. Many companies sold wattage right off the trolley wire, and often it was the only electric power available to rural users. For one dollar a year and the promise of a stop on the farmer's property, car lines could get easements for their tracks, wire, and poles, and farmers bought hundreds of dollars worth of advance tickets or company bonds to help finance the lines.

When the electric's high-pressure salesmen did encounter an intractable farmer, the company simply skirted his property, curving the track out to the road and back on the other side of his pasture. The

Cleveland & Eastern Traction Co. secured right-of-way along the edge of a property belonging to the Methodist Church by providing the church with a steeple bell. A Gates Mills, Ohio, lawyer named Harrison B. McGraw tells how he eventually overcame the resistance of a determined landowner who had threatened him with a shotgun: "I discontinued negotiations at once," said Mr. McGraw. McGraw was the only lawyer the landowner knew, and hostile as he may have been, he was obliged a short while later to ask the attorney to represent his wife in a dispute with a piano-moving company. Fortunately for the line and Mr. McGraw, the lady won, and the shotgun-toter ceded easement to the trolley line.

Light interurbans like this one were once a familiar sight in northern New England. Photograph by Joseph B. Doherty. Courtesy of John Stern.

The interior of a high-speed interurban car in 1903. Illustration from *The Electric Railway Dictionary*, courtesy of Newton K. Gregg.

Warmth with elegance. This coal stove could burn hastily gathered twigs in a pinch. Illustration from *The Electric Railway Dictionary*, courtesy of Newton K. Gregg.

Perhaps the most extreme instance of traction company meddling was when the Chicago and Wheaton Electric Railway, on August 3, 1901, induced Mrs. Amelia J. Hoover to get a divorce from the husband from whom she had been separated for seventeen years, in order to clear title to a right-of-way.

Once inside an interurban car, riders could choose a seat covered in plush or leather in the main section, or one covered with rattan in the smoking section. Here a man could enjoy his cigar or cigarette without offending the lady riders; a sliding door segregated the smokers. As often as not, he could join a game of penny ante, or simply chat with his fellow passengers.

Highly polished hardwoods—mahogany, cherry, oak—paneled the interior of the earlier interurban cars. Sometimes hand-carved wooden moldings further embellished the vehicle's interior, and the brass fittings—handles, doorknobs, window hardware—were consciously graceful in design. Later, decoration gave way to function and interiors became more severe.

In cold weather, a coal stove, stoked by the conductor, heated water, which circulated in pipes running along the walls. Electric heating not only would have diverted power from the important business of running the trolleys, but in case of a winter power failure could well be the cause of the stranded occupants freezing to death. With a coal stove, being stranded in the cold for a long period simply meant that when the coal gave out the male passengers and the crew went into the countryside to pick up wood.

Overhead racks accommodated hand luggage; cars on longer runs had a ten-foot baggage compartment behind the motorman. On any trip scheduled for more than an hour, the law required a toilet. It usually occupied a tiny but elegant cubicle about the size of a phone booth in the center of the car. Steam road facilities, such as sleeping cars and diners, were superfluous on the shorter interurban lines, although in 1907 the Illinois Traction Company (later the Illinois Terminal Railway) tried providing sleepers for the passengers on longer trips out of St. Louis. The service was not highly successful, and the line soon converted most of the berths to ordinary seats.

Travelers who expected to get hungry while riding packed their own food. They could supplement their bag lunches with the candy butcher's wares—sandwiches, apples, candy, Cracker Jack, chewing gum, salted peanuts, Hershey almond bars, and cigars. Air conditioning was years away, but there were shades and even curtains to shield the riders from the sun; and if they wanted air, they could open the windows without encountering clouds of smoke, cinders, and soot. The electrics were clean.

"People think trolley cars are all alike," said Captain Herbert Dosey of Cleveland, as I sat in his living room surrounded by eight fat scrapbooks of trolley pictures and an old car factory catalog.

"Look through that catalogue," he urged. "They're just as different as houses are!" I could see that they were. They varied in size, in shape, in design. The windows were of many proportions, and some had fanlight upper sashes, rectangular ones of various dimensions; some had none at all. There were deck roofs—a clerestory with straight vertical sides and small ventilator windows; railroad roofs, where the clerestory ends were curved down for streamlining; arch roofs, a completely curved roof with no clerestory. Doors were at the end or in the middle; there was, or there was not, a dropped platform. The wheel trucks were set under the car at varying distances from the

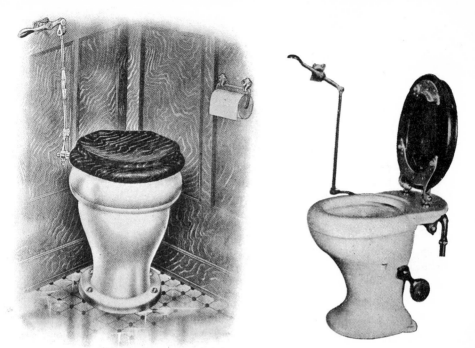

Trips that took longer than an hour made certain comforts necessary. Illustration from *The Electric Railway Dictionary*, courtesy of Newton K. Gregg.

ends, depending upon the sharpness of the corners and curves that the car had to negotiate. Captain Dosey told me that, in addition to looking different, each model differed from the others in the particular specifications it met, and these were dictated by the number of passengers they would carry, the speed at which they would run, the frequency, the grades they would have to climb, the length of the run, and the height of any overhead obstructions. City cars, interurban cars, and steam railroad trains were ordinarily built to a standard gauge, however—4 feet 8½ inches.

Commercial jealousy often influenced a company's choice of interurban car design. "At one time," said Dosey, "there was such rivalry between car companies that Pomeroy and Mandelbaum's Cleveland, Southwestern wouldn't buy a style of car if it had been ordered by Everett and Moore's Northern Ohio Traction and Light."

Whatever the design of the car, it was painted according to the buyer's wishes, and the distinctive colors of the different lines were called their livery. Pullman green was popular and so was dark green, frequently with a yellow letterboard. Several lines used red livery,

BRILL CONVERTIBLE CAR (PATENTED), WITH "NARRAGANSETT" SILL STEPS. MOUNTED ON BRILL "EUREKA" MAXIMUM-TRACTION TRUCKS (PATENTED)

Length over end panels, 30' 5½"
Length over vestibules, 40' 9½"
Length of platforms, 5' 2"
Width over sills (Z iron), 7' 8½"
Width over posts at belt, 7' 11¼"
Height from floor to ceiling, 8' 5½"

Height from under side of side sills over trolley board, 9' 6½"
Height from track over trolley-board, 11' 11½"
Centers of posts, 2' 6½"
Sweep of posts, 4½"
Thickness of corner posts, 3¾"
Thickness of side posts, 3½"

Side sills (Z iron), 8" x 6" x 4"
End sills, 4¾" x 8"
Length of seats, 34"
Width of aisle, 18¼"
Weight of carbody, 15,000 lbs.
Weight of car and trucks (without motors), 23,300 lbs.

See Dictionary of Electric Railway Materials for Descriptions of Cars and Trucks

See Dictionary of Electric Railway Materials for Descriptions of Cars and Trucks

Length over end panels, 30' 8"
Length over vestibules, 41' 8"
Length of platforms, 5' 6"
Width over sills, 8' ½"
Width over posts at belt, 8' 4"
Height from floor to ceiling, 8' 4"

Height from under side of side sills over trolley board, 9' 3¼"
Height from track over trolley board, 12' ½"
Centers of posts, 2' 8"
Sweep of posts, 1¾"
Thickness of corner posts, 3¾"
Thickness of side posts, 3½"
Side sills, 4" x 7¾"

Sill plates, 12" x ¾"
End sills, 5½" x 6¾"
Length of seats, 36"
Width of aisle, 24"
Weight of carbody, 18,200 lbs.
Weight of car and trucks (without motors), 28,200 lbs.

CITY TYPE OF BRILL SEMI-CONVERTIBLE CAR (PATENTED), WITH "DETROIT" PLATFORMS. MOUNTED ON BRILL NO. 27-G TRUCKS (PATENTED)

The combination car transferred to the open streetcar of fond memory in summer. The semiconvertible opened up to the warm breezes, but not all the way. *Electric Railway Journal*, 1906.

with various letterboard colors—cream, blue, or yellow. The Cleveland, Southwestern cars were painted light green, and the company advertised itself as The Green Line, while the largest Pacific Electric trolleys were known as The Big Red Cars. The orange juice color that so many people associate with trolley cars was the most popular, for safety reasons: it contrasted with summer's green and winter's white and was known as "traction orange."

A few weeks after meeting Captain Dosey, I visited another railfan, a man in his early thirties who knew the interurbans only after the fact. This young man, whose name is James Businger, is by profession a model builder, making demonstration models of farm machinery and the like for such companies as United States Steel. While he, too, owns model interurban cars, Mr. Businger is a "hardware collector." He has (along with a vast knowledge of the trolley industry) a fantastic collection of interurban artifacts, from conductors' coat buttons to pieces of the side paneling from trolley cars. He has lanterns, headlights, interior lights, early bulbs, three-note brass whistles, bells, controllers, destination boards, pieces of window glass—he

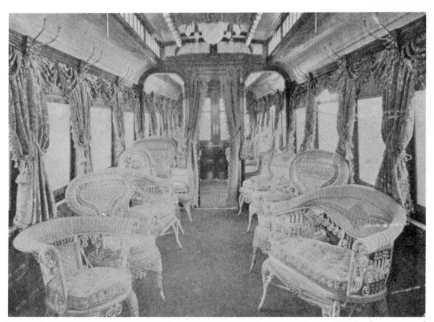

The luxurious interior of an early interurban parlor car (about 1904). Courtesy of the Picture Collection, The Branch Libraries, The New York Public Library.

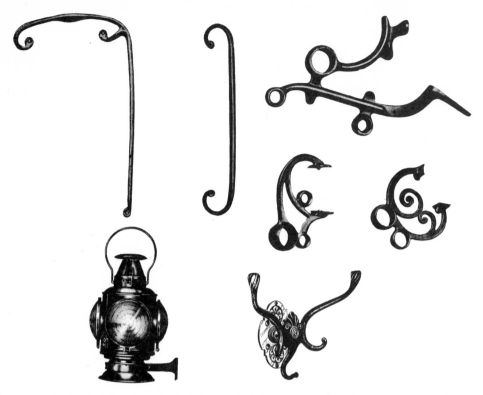

In 1911, interurban car builders took it for granted that the solid brass hardware would be made to look graceful as well as practical. Illustrations from *The Electric Railway Dictionary*, courtesy of Newton K. Gregg.

apologized for the lack of order in his collection, explaining that he had just moved and hadn't had a chance to set up his model track to put things in their places. It seemed neatly disposed to me, and I had the feeling that if someone were to blow a whistle, all the parts would leap together and a fully equipped interurban car would materialize in Mr. Businger's basement.

He offered me a seat in a plush-upholstered chair that looked a great deal like one of those charming Victorian round-back side chairs, but which tipped alarmingly when I leaned forward to look at a picture he held out. "Be careful!" he cried. "I haven't had a chance to bolt that to the floor yet." I discovered that I was sitting in what had been one of the twenty-five chairs in an interurban parlor car, a car which, because of its limited seating, was deplored by Mr. Businger as being sadly uneconomic.

"The men who built the car bodies," he said, "were cabinetmakers. Look at this!" He handed me a large piece of the exterior side panel of a car—just an ordinary wooden interurban car. It was smooth as glass, highly varnished, with the grain carefully brought out. The early cars were built, like fine pieces of furniture, of woods such as cherry, oak, and mahogany. Later, lighter steel cars supplanted the wooden ones, and still later some cars were made of aluminum. Ironically, when the metal cars came out, many companies tried to camouflage their wooden trolleys to look like metal.

Inlaid in the wood, as was customary, was a strip of lighter wood put there simply for decoration. The lettering on the outside of both city and interurban cars was of gold leaf, and there were itinerant artists who decorated the cars with designs from nature—sheaves of wheat or corn, garlands of wild roses, maple leaves. These traveling painters were also responsible for the elaborate gold designs on old fire engines.

All the metalwork on the car—door and window hardware, rails, handholds, controllers, whistles, bells, headlights, even the switch keys the conductors carried, were of brass. The window of the toilet cubicle and often the upper sashes and the clerestory windows were glazed with stained glass, frequently of the type where the colors are swirled together in a sort of rainbow ice-cream effect. This was not only esthetic. In the toilets, the stained glass afforded privacy; in the upper sashes, shade from the sun. The colored glass clerestory evolved from the early trolley lines, where in many instances it was the way the segment of riders who were illiterate could recognize the car they wanted to take.

At first, the plug-in incandescent light bulbs with their large coiled filaments were considered so beautiful to look upon that they were left unshaded. The Montreal sightseeing car, beautifully preserved in the Connecticut Electric Railway Museum at Warehouse Point, and its sister in the Seashore Trolley Museum in Kennebunkport, Maine, have arches adorned with bare bulbs all down the length of the car. When light bulbs became a commonplace sight, the cars blossomed forth with glass lampshades vaguely resembling flowers.

The brass signal lanterns that hung on the back of the car had red, yellow, green, and white reflectors, and the conductor turned to the proper color to signal the cars behind him.

Whistles, operated on the compressed air that activated the brakes,

Stained glass in the upper sashes and the clerestory windows kept the sun out and gave a pleasant glow to the interior. Photograph courtesy of Frances G. Scott.

were necessarily loud, but harmonious. Made up of three brass pipes, they sounded a three-note chord at crossings and other potential encounters. The huge headlamps with two reflectors—white for clear nights, golden for foggy ones—were too bright for city running, and the car carried two reflectorless bulbs beneath the large one to illuminate urban streets.

The early interurban cars had the beauty of functionalism. They were straightforward in their lines and basic construction, and nothing was there that didn't need to be. The rounded front ends had a purpose: they made it easier to turn corners and avoid obstructions when running in urban streets. The curved sides of some cars—called "Cincinnati cars" after the company that made them—added to their strength.

Double headlight on a Connecticut Company car. The upper light was the very bright beam used in country running. Too bright for city streets, it was replaced by the smaller light below when running in town. Photograph courtesy of Frances G. Scott.

The "anticlimber." The horizontally ribbed metal strip at the bottom of this Chicago, North Shore & Milwaukee heavy interurban was a safety device. In a collision, it prevented the trolley from plowing into the interior of the car it hit. Photograph courtesy of Frances G. Scott.

A West Penn Railway flatcar, loaded with rails. Photograph by H. Davis, courtesy of 35 Slides Company, Colorado Springs, Colorado.

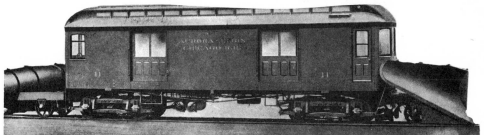

The sweeper brushed away moderate snowfalls. When the snow was heavy, a plow was needed. And when it wasn't going to snow, the plow blade came off and presto—a baggage car. Illustration from *The Electric Railway Dictionary*, courtesy of Newton K. Gregg.

On the front of the interurbans was an arrangement of wooden strips called a "roof mat." It protected the car (and the passengers) if, as sometimes happened, the trolley pole came slamming down onto the roof; otherwise it might break clear through. The "pilot" was a cow (and child, dog, and drunk) catcher, and the "anti-climber" protected a car from being overridden and broken into by the end of another car in a collision. Oil lamps on the rear were not an anachronism in an electric car; if the power was lost they still burned to signal to an unsuspecting motorman following behind.

Under the car, metal rods called "truss rods" could be tightened to keep the sides from sagging with age. Early experiments and experience with city streetcars had taught car builders that the motor should go below the car, attached to the axle. On a single-truck car—a car with but one wheel truck, comprising two wheels to a side, or four wheels altogether—one motor was attached to each of the two axles. On double-truck cars there still was usually no need for more than two motors, so two 125 hp motors were connected to the axles of one truck. It was possible, of course, to motorize both trucks, and if this was necessary, it was done. A box motor, which both carried freight and pulled a string of motorless trailer boxcars, was frequently equipped with the entire 500 hp.

Herbert Dosey explained the reason for dividing the power source between two or four motors. "When a 500 hp motor is needed in an industrial application, it is a simple matter to build a concrete base, mount a 500 hp motor, and connect it to the load. The physical size of the motor is rarely critical. But the space beneath a railway car is approximately four feet between the wheels. At least four inches of clearance is needed above rail height, and the space between the axle and the truck bolster is also a fixed dimension. So, to power a car with 500 hp, four 125 hp motors would be the answer."

Captain Dosey also explained that the gearing, depending upon the topography of the line, would have a ratio of about three to one.

"The motors," said Captain Dosey, "would rotate three times while the car wheels made one complete turn." He said that the Lake Shore Electric, a major interurban railroad with which he was connected many years ago, had a ratio of 21:57, which means that the motor gear had 21 teeth, the larger axle gear 57. "This," he pointed out for the benefit of those who, like me, can't do quick sums in their head, "is close to a 3:1 ratio."

In addition to regular rolling stock, the railway companies had

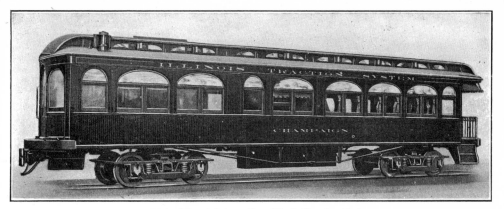

Fig. 176—Officers' Private Car; Illinois Traction System
The J. G. Brill Company, Builder

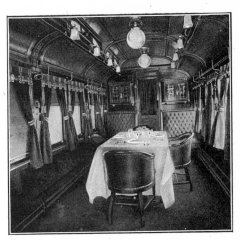

Fig. 177—Observation Room of Private Car Shown   Fig. 178—Dining Room of Private Car Shown in
in Fig. 176   Fig. 176

The J. G. Brill Company, Builder

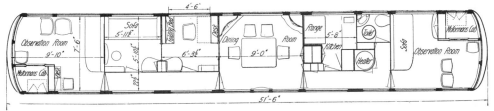

Fig. 179—Floor Plan of Private Car; Milwaukee Electric Railway & Light Company
St. Louis Car Company, Builder

(51)

A traveling office, the officers' car of the Illinois Traction Company. Illustrations
from *The Electric Railway Dictionary*, courtesy of Newton K. Gregg.

special cars built or furnished for specific functions. There were, of course, the work cars—a line car, with a platform on its roof from which linemen could work on the trolley wires; crane cars (for laying track, principally); and emergency cars. For clearing snow off the track, the lines used either a snow sweeper, a car with an extra motor that operated revolving brooms, or, for areas where heavier storms and more rugged terrain demanded more rugged equipment, the heavier plows. These had big shear plows mounted on a pair of "pony" wheels and protruding from the front of the car. The railways soon realized that there was a disadvantage to having a lot of money tied up in snow-removing apparatus "which is idle from nine to ten months in the year, during which it occupies valuable space in the car-barns," as one official of the Chicago, Aurora and Elgin wrote. They therefore specified cars with removable snow shears and seats that could be installed easily, thus turning the snowplow into an express or freight car in the months when snow was light and travel heavy.

The officials of the line usually commanded a private car, an extra-luxurious one that was the last word in Victorian glory. These cars were painted a special color and bore a name rather than a number, often the name of the president's wife. They were paneled inside, with handcarved oak woodwork and scrollwork and mirrors. Brass spittoons gleamed between the upholstered armchairs, and the floor was carpeted with broadloom. Cut-glass lamps and fixtures lit the interior. The car was furnished with movable furniture of high quality; not only chairs but tables, sideboards, and plant stands contributed to the executives' comfort. Lace curtains and silk window blinds alternated with gilded vases of flowers along the wall. There was a galley where the steward could prepare refreshments to be served along the way, and the motorman was separated from his betters in a glass-enclosed platform. Henry E. Huntington, who built the Pacific Electric Railway on the West Coast, had a wood-burning fireplace in his private car. These cars were for the owners' pleasure and convenience. They were used, too, to impress important stockholders, current or prospective, who frequently were carried in them on a tour of the holdings.

One such was *Josephine,* the private car of Henry A. Everett of the Everett-Moore syndicate in Cleveland. One of the earliest private cars (it was built in 1903) *Josephine* had a smoking room at one end furnished with half a dozen leather chairs. An observation room with easy chairs and a sofa was at the other end. Between them were a toilet with a hot-water heater and a linen closet, a complete office, and a stateroom with a brass bed and washbasin. *Josephine* was dark green on the outside, mahogany-paneled inside, and had a light green ceiling. There were green draperies, curtains, and rugs, and the decorator touch was carried over to the china and glassware, the linen, and the accessories.

Trolley car construction was once a sizable business—there were seven big car builders in Ohio alone. They turned out regular rolling stock and various extra-comfort cars. There were parlor and observation cars, dining and buffet cars. The Pacific Electric, in the balmy air of pre-smog Southern California, ran a number of cars that were half open and half closed, and there were many combinations of styles. Three interurban lines carried sleepers, although this was most unusual.

Probably the best way yet devised for getting a funeral party to the cemetery was the interurban funeral car, which the family of the deceased could hire for the occasion. Usually a converted and appropriately decorated "combination" car (one with compartments for baggage, smoking, and regular seats), the funeral car had a plush-lined section behind the motorman for the casket, with fold-up racks for floral offerings. The smoking compartment was fitted out with wicker chairs for the bereaved family. Between the family compartment and the main section of the car were the heater and "rest room facilities," and the remainder of the car accommodated the other mourners on the inevitable funeral folding chairs. The Cleveland, Southwestern & Columbus Railway's funeral car was aptly named *Dolores*. Max Wilcox, a railfan whose interest in the interurbans is so encompassing and compelling that it has several times broken out in print, describes the *Dolores* in his privately issued book on the Cleveland, Southwestern.

> *Dolores* was painted dark blue with gold lettering, striping and numerals. Behind the motorman's vestibule was a plush-lined compartment, with the doors opening outward. Rollers mounted in the floor made it easy to roll the casket in. [It was] then strapped into place. . . . The interior decor was beautifully finished in grey oak woodwork, dark blue curtains and drapes, blue plush seats, with dark blue carpeting on the floor.

Descanso (Rest), a funeral car that was used in southern California. Photograph by Jim Walker. Courtesy of the Orange Empire Railway Museum.

In these cars the entire mourning party—and the deceased as well—went to the cemetery together, instead of stringing out along the highway in an obstructionist line of slow-moving automobiles. All this splendor was available at ten to forty dollars for the half day the trip took. Max Wilcox has a record showing that the *Dolores* made forty-five trips in one month. His father Ed, motorman, conductor, and trainmaster on the Cleveland, Southwestern & Columbus Railway for thirty years and now nearly ninety, remembers four funerals on the *Dolores* in one day.

Out west, where homes and towns were far apart, interurbans ran special school trains, and it was this practice that led to the formation of consolidated schools. In fact, the only regularly scheduled passenger trains on one branch of the Utah-Idaho Central Railroad were two such school trains.

It was common for interurban lines to carry sealed mailbags from one community to another. More complex—and more interesting—were the rail post offices. These were sections of cars that served as traveling post offices. (There were, and probably still are, RPOs on the railroads, but the trolley post offices had a charm of their own.) Jim Businger has a yellowing postcard dated 1910 with the postmark "Trolley Rail P.O."

Mail was picked up at the point of departure and at stops along the way, and as the car clacked through the countryside, it was postmarked, sorted, and bagged, and dropped off at local destinations.

The first trial run of a trolley rail post office was authorized in 1891 on a branch of the city trolley line that became the St. Louis and Florissant. The route was eighteen miles long, and it was covered four times a day by a combination RPO–milk car–express. The post office section had a canceling table, a rack for the mail pouches, and a letter case.

The first genuine intercity electric rail post office ran between Rockland and Camden on the Knox County Electric Railway in Maine in 1893.

In 1893 the postal employees who rode the St. Louis cars demonstrated their prowess on the move by collecting a letter, sorting it and its companion pieces, transmitting and delivering it to a typical address—all in less than an hour from the time it was mailed. At that time, the RPO was handling 1,000 pounds of mail per trip.

The Indiana Railroad was an important RPO line, carrying mail from Indianapolis to Peru, some seventy-six miles, in a 61-foot-long passenger car with a 15-foot mail compartment separated from the passenger section by solid walls with only "creep" doors—doors which my trolley enthusiast friend Blair Foulds, who has ridden these cars, calls "doghouse doors." They are just two feet high, cut into the bottom of the partition, and are there to be used only in an emergency.

Similar cars carried and processed the mail between Fort Wayne and New Castle on the Indiana. A postal clerk of that time wrote a description of one of these mail trips—this one in the dead of an Indiana winter. The train left Fort Wayne at 5 A.M. with a huge pile of mail pouches loaded into the RPO—so many that they overflowed into the passenger section. The car careered at 65 mph toward New Castle. Mail messengers waited at spots along the line to make "breakneck" exchanges, taking in the sorted mail, giving the rail postal clerks sacks of letters for destinations farther along the line. The car was so beastly cold that the postmarking ink froze.

The trolley mail story has a familiar postscript: The last RPOs on that pioneer line ran in 1941, when slower buses were substituted for the interurban trolleys. People gathered at every crossroad to watch the cars go by, and village postmasters, says Bryant Long in his book *Mail by Rail*, "brought their last pouches to the car with unashamed tears in their eyes."

The ninety-mile Spokane and Moscow run in Washington State and Idaho carried a poet in the mail compartment, who memorialized his experiences in rhyme:

> It gives the clerk a mighty queer feeling
> As it [the trolley pole] pokes its way through the
> express car ceiling.

The Pacific Electric "big red cars" between San Bernardino and Los Angeles carried mail on RPOs for two years, beginning late—rather astonishingly so—in the life of the industry. It was the last trolley RPO in existence.

Although the interurbans were conceived primarily as passenger lines, most of them also carried freight. An interurban freight train was made up of a box motor (or trolley locomotive). An interurban freight train was made up of a box motor (or trolley locomotive) and one, two, or more freight cars, not motorized, which the box motor (or loco) pulled. The length of the train was limited by the restrictions in various towns and cities through which the line passed; too long a train would tie up traffic at more than one intersection at a time.

If the train was not going to do any street running, it was possible for one trolley locomotive to pull from eight to fifteen cars. In fact, with well-kept, modern (for the time) equipment, electric trolley cars were astonishingly strong. William Heinemann, an atypically peripatetic interurban man who in a forty-eight-year career worked on a number of lines from Ohio to Iowa, told me a story about one of them, the Des Moines & Central Iowa Interurban Railway, that dramatically illustrates the point. That line used to pull the Robinson circus to its winter quarters in Moran, Iowa. The procedure was for the circus train, drawn by two steam locomotives, to make a connection with the DM & CI. A little turtleback engine—a small but powerful machine that was a kind of tugboat of the rails—would then

A box motor. This dual-purpose car pulled a string of trailers without power of their own and also had space to carry freight. Photograph courtesy of Ron Brown.

replace the steam locos and pull the circus train down the line to Moran. In 1911 or 1912 Mr. Heinemann was present when the train puffed in and the interurban crew walked over to the steam men for their waybills. "How you going to take them down there?" demanded the steam road men. "It's an uphill pull. You can't move this train with that thing!"

"Tell you what," said the trolley motorman calmly, in the manner of Babe Ruth pointing to the spot where he was going to hit the next pitch. "I'll take the train and I'll pull both your locomotives with it." He did.

Hauling comparatively small loads of freight, the interurbans could compete with the steam roads because they gave direct service. A steam road car full of roller bearings bound from Cleveland to Detroit took four days or more in transit, what with being shunted off at yards on the way and routed here and there to accommodate the other shipments on the train. The Lake Shore Electric, with a freight running time of about nine hours between the two cities, delivered the machine

Freight running was forbidden in some cities; others limited the hours freight could run and the size of the trains. In some, it was necessary to camouflage the freight car to look like a passenger car. But here is an interurban freight train unabashedly at large in the streets of a midwest city (probably Fort Wayne, Indiana). Photograph by Frank W. Schlegel, courtesy of Blair Foulds.

parts in one day. A load of freight almost always went from its pickup point to its destination virtually nonstop. When automobile production stepped up in the twenties, an interurban three-car freight ran every twenty minutes from Akron to Detroit, loaded with tires from the rubber factories. (The time came, however, when the Ford Motor Company refused to accept freight from the electrics, which they thought of as their competitors, and brought trucks over the newly improved roads to fetch their tires from Akron.)

Local freight, of course, was a big part of the business. Produce from farms, merchandise for the smaller towns, all traveled on the electrics. Trolleys were chartered for regular deliveries. The Cleveland *Plain Dealer* paid fifty dollars a day each for cars that took the daily out of Cleveland—on Sunday they paid more for larger cars to carry the larger paper. The crew could expect to find regular (and apparently compulsive) readers waiting for the Sunday paper at each stop. Others, townspeople with more basic concerns, met the beer car that brought the draught from Cleveland breweries to the thirsty countryside.

Leon George worked a special freight nightly for eight months when the Youngstown plant of a bakery chain burned down and the interurban instituted a bread run from the chain's Bedford bakery. (Bedford is a town a few miles south of Cleveland.) It left at 1 A.M. every morning, carrying hot loaves of bread; if it arrived in Youngstown later than 4 A.M. the load was refused. On Friday nights the box motor pulled a trailer, carrying Sunday's bread. "That was a busy track," said Mr. George. "There was a mail car out of Cleveland, and a passenger coach, and the bread train from Bedford. And then a freight coming out of Alliance. All about the same time. They sent the mail car first, then the bread car, then the passenger coach and last the freight. All of them were coming hard down the right-of-way and nobody wanted to have to wait for anybody!"

On a milk run, the motorman and conductor wrestled ten-gallon cans, each of which, when filled with milk, weighed eighty-five pounds. Depending on the size of the car, they could carry 100 to 250 cans in each, setting them upright side by side on the floor and putting planking over their tops to support a second layer. Herbert Dosey says the interurbans brought 20,000 gallons of milk into Cleveland daily; there was a freight depot in the center of the city where they could unload fifteen or twenty cars at once.

Freight handlers worked the depots, but the train crew had to take care of the way stops. Coming back, they laid the empty cans on their sides and rolled them out of the car at each milk station. Each dairy farmer had a platform down by the car line on which he set out his milk. According to Ed Wilcox, the platforms were sometimes used for less respectable purposes. He worked with a Don Juanish motorman, one of whose many lady friends was the wife of a dairy farmer on his route. Every midday the fortunate motorman found a hot pie waiting for him on the milk stand.

While a good bit of interurban freight was of the crate-of-celery, basket-of-plums variety, there were some complicated runs. One trolley train picked up steel from Pittsburgh at Harmony, Pennsylvania (an unusual difference in gauge kept the train from going all the way into Pittsburgh); the steel was bound for Atlanta, Georgia, on a four-day schedule. The cars were routed northwest, through Silver Lake Junction outside of Akron on to Cleveland on the ABC line.

There a Lake Shore Electric motor took them farther west to Toledo. From Toledo the car went on the Cincinnati & Lake Erie track to Cincinnati, then on the track of the steam road, the Louisville & Nashville, to Atlanta. On the way back, empty, the cars were routed on steam road tracks to Chicago, loaded with meat, and brought back to Cleveland on the rails of the steam Nickel Plate Railroad. One car of meat was dropped off in Cleveland, and then, running on ABC track once more, the trolley brought the rest of the meat back to Akron.

Interurban freight business varied. Some lines carried freight on their own tracks only. Many interchanged with other companies, cars of one line being picked up and included in trains of another. The most profitable had interchange arrangements with the steam roads.

Piggyback freight hauling, which is the transfer of an entire truck trailer to a rail flatcar, is relatively new on the railroads today, but it was an interurban practice as early as 1894–1895. A California interurban at that time carried express wagons on flatcars to Oakland, where they went on to San Francisco by ferry. When Martin Ackerman was on the Lake Shore Electric extra list, he worked on the "Bonner Railwagon." This was a device that brought a truck equipped with a special trailer to the trolley line. The trailer had, in addition to its two rubber-tired back wheels, two extra wheels in the front, which were of flanged metal and were retractable. With these wheels down, the bodies were pushed up a ramp and the flatcar backed under them. A sixty-five-foot flatcar carried three rail wagons between a point west of Cleveland and the outskirts of Toledo, and eliminated many miles of trolley street-running in those cities.

In many cases, it was the freight business that kept an interurban line going for a significant time after passenger traffic had dwindled to almost nothing. In addition to regular freight, some companies did an express business that provided drayage to haul the cargo to and from the trolley stop, and the slogan "express service at freight rates" became a cliché. In Cleveland the five lines that entered the city in 1894 cooperated to form a highly profitable express agency, which they called the Electric Package Company. It carried on a successful delivery service until the last line, the Lake Shore Electric, closed down in 1938.

Probably the most forward-looking interurban management was the Cass family of the Waterloo, Cedar Falls & Northern Railroad in

Iowa. They, unlike many interurban managers, campaigned actively to get interchanges with the steam and Diesel roads. As a result, in the 1920s, when interurbans were falling right and left, the WCF&N was making more money each year. As late as 1944 the road had its most profitable year. But there was still too small a margin over operating costs to continue competing with regular railroads and truck lines, and the WCF&N had to close down a few years later.

3
An Interurban to Anywhere

As soon as the interurbans were built, the public joyfully began to ride them. They rode them to visit grandmother sixty miles away, to call on a girl in the next town, to take the family out of the city for a daylong picnic. Children rode down the line to buy fresh eggs and sweet corn, lawyers visited clients, doctors took patients into the city hospitals. It was inexpensive and convenient for groups to charter special cars—when Oberlin played football with Ohio State in Columbus, the school hired ten trolley cars to carry 650 students to the game. The team, of course, went by interurban too. The Midwest is sprinkled with small colleges, and the trolleys made possible a busy schedule of intramural basketball, debates, glee club concerts, track meets, and just plain get-togethers.

The interurban trolleys were an active part of the community, and they played an intimate role in the daily life of the people, a role that the trainmen were pleased to have a part in. James Businger, among his thousands of mementos, cherishes a trolley pass with a grocery list on the back of it; there was time during a layover for the motorman or conductor to do some errands for a housewife on the route, and neither the housewife nor the trainman thought of it as an imposition. It was common to put children on the cars, telling the conductor to let them off at "stop 38," or wherever, there to be met by a grandparent or aunt. The conductors would see that they *were* met, too; if the grandparent hadn't shown up, something was done about it.

Slightly older children rode the cars by themselves, taking messages or parcels to relatives, bringing Pa's lunch to him, nice and hot, on the job, or making for nearby farms or country stores to pick up fresh butter at twenty cents a pound or a dressed chicken for sixty-five cents.

"You could do something for people," a delightful and articulate gentleman named Ward Platt told me with satisfaction. Mr. Platt is a former conductor on the Lake Shore Electric. "Here's a man that gets on at some stop, the same stop, the same car every morning. Well, if one morning he wasn't there, you'd look down the street. If you saw him running, you'd wait for him. If he wasn't in sight, the motorman would start blowing the whistle, banging the bell, to let him know the car was there." Only when this racket didn't produce the commuter did the trolley man assume that he was indisposed or for some other reason not riding his regular car that day.

Even as now, commuters played cards on the ride to the office, although the game was more likely to be pinochle or poker than bridge. The conductor held their regular seats in the smoking room for the players and furnished a destination board marked "charter" to serve as a table. Regular riders showed their gratitude with ties, cigars, and whiskey for Christmas. Mr. Platt had a passenger, a wealthy Cleveland lawyer, who lived in the countryside west of Vermilion,

Drenwood, Pennsylvania, on the Altoona & Logan Valley line. Photograph courtesy of 35 Slides, Colorado Springs, Colorado.

Ohio. The right-of-way ran across his extensive property, a privilege he had granted in return for having any car stop for him near his house. This attorney, Dixon, who regularly rode an early morning trolley, raised peaches as a gentleman's hobby. "You've never seen such peaches," Mr. Platt said, still overcome by their perfection forty or fifty years later. "A-1 they were. His trees were so well kept and so well pruned that when you looked out of the car at them it looked as though you could walk right across the tops of the trees! Well, every morning during the peach season that man would give a peck basket of peaches to the conductor and to the motorman. 'What are we going to do with all those peaches?' we'd ask him. 'Have your wife can them,' he'd say." I wondered how Mrs. Platt felt about having a peck of peaches handed to her every day for weeks, with the obligation of canning them at once or letting them rot.

The trolley men delivered packages, too, for small-town merchants and for individuals. "Ward," somebody would say, "I need a new tire for my car. I have to get it from Kelly Sieberling in Cleveland—it's an odd size. If I call them they'll get it down to the terminal this morning, and you bring it up here." Charles Peters told me that he delivered prescriptions from Cleveland pharmacies to houses along his route, and there was a brisk traffic in homelier items —dress patterns, a cake for a married daughter down the line, a pipe forgotten at a friend's house on the last visit. "But then," said Ward Platt, "the company got smart, and started doing it themselves and charging for it. They called it 'Parcel Dispatch,' and they made a real good thing out of it. Of course, you couldn't ask for quicker service."

The interurbans made an enormous difference to farmers and, more particularly, to farmers' wives, who now could go off to the city for a day's shopping. Traveling salesmen, visiting one small store after another in the numerous communities the interurbans touched, found their territories almost magically expanded, as they abandoned buggies and stages and the infrequent local steam trains to ride the electrics. If their wares or samples were of manageable size, they also carried bicycles with them, stowing them in the baggage compartment or tying them on the trolley's fender, and riding them through the streets of each town they covered.

"The good thing about the trolleys," said an elderly former salesman, "was that you could go to all kinds of little towns and, later in the day, when you'd made your sales call and were ready to leave, there was certain to be another car along soon."

Out-of-town interurban stations came in all shapes and sizes. Albany and Hudson Railroad Company, Albany Electric Park, ca. 1909.

City residents began buying summer property along lake shores or in the countryside; land near the Great Lakes jumped as much as ten times in value when the interurbans opened the area. Many of these new colonies were within an easy trolley ride of the city, and families soon discovered that they could have the pleasures of lakefront or country living all year around, while Father rode the trolley to the office each day. A few managements, recognizing that people with money were often happy to spend it for privilege, put on extra fare cars. Mr. J. N. Fleming, who in 1943 recalled the early days of the Cleveland exurban village of Gates Mills, tells of the "bankers' limited," which ran morning and evening for the business and professional men of the village. "Monthly tickets were sold at a slight premium for the rides on this 'limited,' " he wrote. "All the members of the family were privileged to ride on it, but were required to hold up a yellow ticket as they stood at an uptown corner after shopping; otherwise the motorman would not stop. A very friendly and jolly group of businessmen rode into Cleveland each morning. The morning papers came out on an early car, and were available to those who wished to read, but most of them chatted and debated how those at Washington should act." (Gates Mills is still a fashionable Cleveland suburb, but the businessmen now ride to town in unfriendly isolation in their automobiles, bucking a crowded freeway at some ultimate sacrifice of their jollity.)

Indiana Railroad's #202, now running at the California Railroad Museum in Rio Vista, once kept the midwest's commerce going. Photograph by John Stern.

In this period, in spite of the panics of 1903 and 1907, industry was rapidly developing in the Midwest, and factory owners were anxious for the wider labor market they could draw on if an interurban line ran to their plant. Some of them even put up money for extensions or spurs of an existing line. Mr. F. J. Meyers, of the Meyers Pump Company, financed a 37-mile section of the Cleveland, Southwestern from Seville, Ohio, to his plant at Mansfield. (The company then made farmers' sink pumps; it is still in business in Mansfield, manufacturing huge electrical pumps for industry.) Mr. Kolp, of the Hoover Vacuum Cleaner Company in Canton, started a trolley line from there to Cleveland in competition with Everett and Moore's ABC line, but he became discouraged with the idea before construction was finished, and Everett-Moore's NOTL took over the completed section.

A one-time mayor of Cleveland named Tom L. Johnson, a compelling political figure whose statue now stands in Cleveland's Public Square, was responsible for the trolley that brought workers to a steel plant in Lorain, Ohio. (He was also responsible for the steel plant, which is now a part of United States Steel.) It was known locally as the

"Old Johnson 3-fare line," because "the conductor held out his hand three times during the run, getting three cents each time."

William Heinemann during his long career has been master mechanic, power superintendent, chief electrician, and construction superintendent, and during the First World War he was employed at the Gary, Indiana, steel plant. There he was responsible for getting 8,000 people in and out of the plant area three times a day. It was during his stay in Gary that Mr. Heinemann took forty cars of people in one train from South Bend to the Great Lakes Naval Training Station near Chicago, an obviously impossible feat of logistics, which perhaps helps to explain his successful career. Contrary to the proverb, this particular rolling stone gathered considerable moss, and ended as general superintendent of the Shaker Rapid, a rapid transit system built by the fabulous Van Sweringen brothers to enhance the value of the real estate they owned in suburban Shaker Heights.

Special cars carried baseball fans into cities like Cleveland, Cincinnati, Pittsburgh, and Detroit from far out in the surrounding countryside every time the home team played. The trolleys went directly to the ball park and waited patiently there until the game was over, whereupon they took the rooters back home again. There were even Trolley League teams, with local supporters following their own particular team around the circuit on the car lines.

Interurbans even had a wheel in the glamorous world of the movies. In *Mayer & Thalberg, The Make-Believe Saints* (Random House, 1975), Samuel Marx tells how in 1930 producer Irving Thalberg, by renting a Pacific Electric trolley car for the evening, was able to assure himself that the audience at his secret sneak previews were truly the general public and not Hollywood know-it-alls. If the car alone cost $400 for the trip—well, the studio had the money.

The evening of the preview, one of the Pacific Electric's "Big Red" trolleys would roll up the special spur track on the MGM lot. (The spur was installed after Thalberg held so many secret previews that everyone decided it would be worthwhile.) Studio executives, summoned to the event by a phone call that morning from the publicity office, boarded the car, with Thalberg always last. While they traveled to a destination known only to him and to the trolley crew, the movie people played bridge in the specially appointed front section of the trolley, and ate and drank a collation served by a waiter from the studio commissary. The trolley took them to Santa Ana, or to Riverside, or even the sixty miles to San Bernardino. When the

ULME
BY
GRAV

ULMER PARK

DANCING PAVILION

ULMER PARK
PIC-NIC GROUND

The only
FAMILY RESORT
on LONG ISLAND reached from
NEW YORK by ULMER
ELEVATED TRAINS from BROOKLY

Ulmer Park, Gravesend, Brooklyn, New York, was a typical trolley park. Courtesy of the Picture Collection, The Branch Libraries, The New York Public Library.

picture was over, the car, which had been waiting on a siding near the movie house, carried the guests back to the lot.

People who didn't especially want to go anywhere rode the trolleys just for fun; a pleasant ride through the countryside on a sunny Sunday afternoon or a hot evening was a treat for courting couples or whole families.

The trolley companies actively encouraged pleasure riding. In the spring, Cleveland & Eastern cars carried banners reading "Come to Gates Mills for Wild Flowers! The woods are full of them!"

"Then," continue a Gates Mills couple, reminiscing in 1943 for the benefit of the local historical society, "to the distress of the nature lovers, the city folk came in large numbers, and the paths from the woods to the trolley were strewn with bunches of withered wood treasures—trilliums, hepatica, squirrel corn—and thus began the depletion of our beautiful woods.

"Later followed women picking blackberries . . . then came the 'mushroomers,' mostly foreign men. As the supply was limited and early morning the best time to gather them, they took the last car at night and stayed on the platform of stop 20 for the night, laughing and talking until dawn. One night it was rather cold and they built a fire to keep warm. Rather stupidly, we thought, they built it on the wooden platform, and this started a fire. When they discovered what they had done there was a great deal of excitement and running hither and yon for water to extinguish the fire."

Trips to natural excursion spots like beaches and ice-skating ponds were an obvious source of trolley revenue. The Lake Shore Electric, one of the most substantial lines in the country, ran from Cleveland to Detroit through Sandusky and Toledo. Sandusky has a peninsula into Lake Erie, at the end of which is an amusement park and bathing beach called Cedar Point, and Mr. Platt told me that in 1916 or thereabouts he worked seventeen and one-half hours a day for all of a three-day Fourth of July weekend, taking "trippers" from Cleveland and its suburbs to Cedar Point and other lake beaches. "We'd pack 125 people in one car," he said (the cars had seats for 50 or 60). "They didn't mind the squeeze; they were glad to get aboard." In cooperation with other transport the Cleveland, Southwestern ran an excursion to Niagara Falls at a real bargain price: for only $7.25 a round trip, you could go from anywhere on the line, which had almost 300 miles of track, to Cleveland, then by boat to Buffalo, and from there, on another interurban trolley line, the International Railway, to the Falls.

Crowds at the trolley stop at Pittsburgh's Kennywood Park, 1907. The woman in the center is keeping her skirt off the track. But what is the man on the right doing? Photograph courtesy of Kennywood Park.

Where no natural attractions existed, the railways often built man-made substitutes. Dance pavilions, outdoor theaters, and band shells attracted passengers to the cars. It was the trolley companies that fostered many "Electric Parks," amusement parks featuring the agreeable novelty of electrically operated rides. Many traction companies were in the business of selling electricity. By drumming up business for the parks, the company collected not only on its trolley line, but on the power with which it supplied the rides.

Some of these amusement parks still exist, or did until very recently. Kennywood Park, outside of Pittsburgh, was built by the Mellon family as an enticing destination for their trolley line from the city. Still Pennsylvania's largest amusement park, Kennywood calls itself "The Nation's Greatest Picnic Park," and by coincidence, it is *my* greatest picnic park! In the late twenties and early thirties, I rode the trolley to Kennywood for our area's annual "school picnic"—a long,

hot, beautiful day that was an orgy of half-price rides, root beer in steins, home-packed lunches in echoing pavilions under old trees, and the trolley ride home to the city with the stars overhead and the orange glow from the steel mills lighting the horizon.

The rural picnic ground was originally called "Kenny's Wood," but Andrew Mellon himself rephrased the name and built for his Monongahela Street Railways a large dance pavilion, electric rides of all kinds, and one of the country's first double roller coasters, "The Racer," which added an element of competition to the thrill of its ups and downs.

During those early years the trip to the suburban site was as much of a thrill as anything the park itself had to offer. The ride on the open-air "summer" streetcar was a real trip through the country for courting couples on a Sunday afternoon.

Kennywood Park was still a trolley park in 1924. Photograph courtesy of Kennywood Park.

It took them to a wooded bluff high above the Monongahela River, and for part of the way up to the top the trolley rounded curves that teetered along the edge of the hillside.

In New England, the Fitchburg, Massachusetts, newspaper in 1902 described a local trolley park:

> The feature of the [rail] road is . . . Whalom Park, on the shores of a beautiful lake three-and-a-quarter miles from Fitchburg . . . . The attractions include an open theatre costing $20,000.00 which has a complete set of stage scenery . . . a hotel known as Whalom Park Inn, and the McKinley Cruiser . . . an electric car man-of-war drawn through the streets in torchlight parades during the fall preceding McKinley's first term of office. . . . After the election the

The "kiddies" enjoying this 1924 ride are taking their grandchildren to Kennywood now. Photograph courtesy of Kennywood Park.

boat was placed on a float at the lake. . . . This boat was made at the shops of the state railway company.

The railway also runs a dance hall . . . in an orderly manner, which is patronized by the best people in the locality. . . .

A woman's building . . . of tasty design . . . contains toilet areas, bedrooms for sick people, cribs for babies . . . a bathing pavilion . . . an electric laundry for drying bathing suits . . . and a figure "8" roller coaster erected last season which cost over $15,000.00. . . . 400,000 people visited the park in the first year.

On a hot July day, a few years ago, I visited Euclid Beach Amusement Park, which expired a year or so later. Spread along the shores of Lake Erie, the park looked as though it hadn't changed since 1910. (Except that the rides featured vehicles resembling airplanes and sports cars, it probably hadn't.) The rides were planted among huge old trees, the rest rooms and picnic pavilions were rambling frame constructions trimmed with wooden latticework and gingerbread. There seemed always to be the far-off sound of calliope music in the air, and hanging in a Ferris wheel over the treetops, looking out over the vast lake, you were suddenly fifty years behind the times—and delighted to be there.

4
The Shortest Distance . . .

The grandest, most grandiose scheme of all was a glorious enterprise called the Chicago–New York Electric Air Line Railroad. Like more exalted visions, the concept of The Air Line appeared to its apostle while he was on the road—on the way, in fact, from New York to Chicago. Alexander C. Miller, a banker and for twenty years an official of the Chicago, Burlington & Quincy (steam) Railroad, was discontentedly riding vaguely westward on the New York Central Railroad sometime around 1904 when he was struck by the fact that after three hours in the train he was farther from Chicago than he had been when he started!

As *The Air Line News*, a paper published by the enterprise, was later to quote, "The straight line wins"—or so Mr. Miller believed. With the simplicity of genius, he thereupon conceived The Air Line, an electric railway that would run on a ruler-straight route between the two cities. He saw it as a double-track road having no grade crossings with the steam lines, no gradients over 1 percent, and no curves that could not be taken at 90 miles an hour. With this sort of planning, he felt, he could guarantee an average speed of 75 miles an hour, and could charge ten dollars for the trip (about half the going rate), and cut about 160 to 230 miles from the various existing steam routes.

Whether the bizarre details of The Air Line's rise and fall were any odder than those associated with many other hastily formed interurban schemes is hard to say. But the scale on which all these eccentricities existed was so large that this line stands out from the rest.

Exactly half of the The Air Line's rolling stock. Photograph courtesy of Blair Foulds.

Miller first took his vision to a friend who was a signal engineer; in this way, he believed, he would be able to back his commercial-financial expertise with that of the technician. The engineer, Jonathan D. Price, pondered the notion for a month and then jumped in.

Because the proposed road would compete with others in existence (the Pennsylvania, the Lake Shore, and the New York Central) and still others being planned, Miller and Price decided there was no point in going to the banks for financing. Instead, they went directly to the public. Through persuasion, enthusiasm, faith, and ignorance, they eventually achieved ten thousand investors and a capitalization of $200 million, of which $25 million was in shares of common stock.

The next step, securing franchises, demanded that Miller and Price take on a good and fast-talking associate, and they found just the man in Colonel (of course!) U. P. Hord. Colonel Hord's primary responsibility was to approach landowners (usually farmers) along the proposed route and secure the right-of-way across their fields and meadows.

Whatever greedy dreams these property owners may have cherished were blown away by the gusts of hot air Colonel Hord circulated. Impressive in a long-skirted coat, broad-brimmed campaign hat, and flowing ascot, the colonel was the very model of one of W. C. Field's smooth-talking grifters. He was so successful in persuading his audience that he almost invariably came away with permission to lay track across the property in exchange for a few shares of Air Line stock *and* with the proceeds of an on-the-spot sale of additional shares.

The Air Line investors were probably the most enthusiastic group of stockholders in history. In droves, they attended regular pep meetings at special campsites throughout the country, and they kept their faith in Miller's vision long after it was inconceivable that anyone in his right mind could.

The camp meetings were partly responsible, but it was *The Air Line News* that kept the pot boiling. This inspirational paper, professionally produced and illustrated with numerous photographs of work in progress and the portrait heads of company officials, maintained a tone of euphoria just a little short of hysteria. Slogans scattered throughout each monthly issue's eight or so pages enjoined its readers " 'Not yet, but soon' spells failure," and (rather lamely in this case) "The present age is the determined age of energy and the drones are not getting along very well." In a regular feature called "The Arithmetic Lesson," the editors pointed out such facts as that nine out of ten tons of coal shoveled into the firebox of a steam locomotive were wasted (except as fuel for the enthusiasm of the followers of the electric way of travel). There were profiles of Miller, Price, and other leaders of the company, and paragraphs triumphantly reporting small victories of electric travel over steam.

One issue featured a long verse telling how, by blindly following a calf track, a winding and inefficient road was created. It ended

> Moral: The moral of this tale is plain
> Let us send our "Air Line" train
> Straight across the continent
> Not follow where some fool calf went
> The twentieth century calls for men
> who dare to leave the "once has been"
> And shunning calf-paths which they see
> Aim straight and sure for "what's to be!"

In 1906 work began on The Air Line. The route, as Miller and his colleagues planned it, was an engineering monstrosity. To cross a minor creek in Indiana, a few miles from their starting point, it was necessary to provide fill for a hollow two miles long. They managed to do it, but it took all the money the line had collected, and this was only the first of hundreds of creeks they would encounter.

As construction went slowly on, and in order to be able to report some income to the stockholders, the directors built an amusement park six miles from Laport, Indiana. "Air Line Park," a more conventional concept than the parent railway, was a success; on a Sunday when the weather was good, the line's two green cars carried as many as 1,200 passengers, at ten cents a round trip.

Share owners were further encouraged by the news that U.S. Steel planned to build a major plant, and the city to serve it, on the route. The plant was built; the city became Gary, Indiana, but it didn't help The Air Line.

Their problems were too immediate and too overwhelming. If an insignificant rivulet like that first creek had necessitated such a heroic construction battle, what was going to happen when the line reached the mountains of Pennsylvania?

Fortunately for everyone but the loyal investors, the problem never had to be faced. The Air Line petered out after having built nineteen-and-a-half miles of track in Indiana, on which for awhile it ran its secondhand wooden cars labeled, wistfully, "Chicago" on one end, "New York" on the other.

5
Acts of Man, Acts of God

Those afflicted with chronological parochialism will be surprised to learn that even in the early days electric cars could achieve the speed of a modern automobile. Every trolley man I have met has told me, either challengingly or as though he, too, found it hard to believe, about a stretch of right-of-way somewhere on his route where the cars could get up to seventy-five or eighty miles an hour; some remembered (accurately) speeds as high as ninety miles an hour. There was a great difference, however, between the actual top running speed of the car, or the fastest stretch on the schedule, and the speed that that same car averaged between terminals. In part it was the conveniently frequent stops that slowed the trolleys, but even more responsible was the street-running in cities and towns. The interurbans not only had to contend with the traffic of bicycles, pedestrians, horsedrawn vehicles, and finally the ever-multiplying automobile, but they also had to fit their speed in with the much slower pace of the city cars. The same trolley that averaged less than thirty miles an hour (and that was considered a good overall speed) was scheduled for—and made—speeds of more than sixty and seventy miles an hour on stretches of country right-of-way.

The lines tried to make up for the considerable delay caused by many stops and street-running by putting in limited service on the more important runs. It took the regular trains of the Lake Shore Electric Railway six hours to go the 120 miles from Cleveland to Toledo, but the Limited, stopping only in the major towns, could still

This Fort Wayne Traction Terminal couldn't match the one in Indianapolis, but a lot of cars went in and out in the good times. Photograph by Neuman Studio, courtesy of Blair Foulds.

cut an hour and forty minutes off that schedule by running past the countless stops in the countryside. The Limited on the Cleveland, Painesville & Ashtabula made only four stops, including the terminal points. (I don't know how many stops there were on the regular run, but directions to a company reunion dinner in a Painesville restaurant described it as being at "Old Stop 71," and this was about halfway down the line.)

Some time around the year 1910, Warren Bicknell, the president of the Lake Shore Electric Railway, decided to race his official car, the *Josephine*, against time from Toledo to Cleveland. A special timetable was set, the substations were checked and output at two of them was pushed from 650 volts to 750 volts. Extra police were stationed in every town the line passed through to keep the tracks clear; there were five good-sized towns and countless villages on the route, in addition to a significant amount of travel in the streets of both Toledo and Cleveland. Although, by the rules, regularly scheduled cars took precedence over extras, in this case it was the other way around; the *Josephine* "ruled the iron." The motorman was one Peck Robinson; he started at a hotel in the center of Toledo called the Boody House, with the "Old Man" standing beside him on the platform, cheering him on.

"Peck started to reverse his handle to slow down, like he always did, for the sharp curve on Rte. 20 near Monroeville," Mr. Heinemann, who saw part of the run from the Monroeville substation, said. "And the Old Man said to him, 'What's the matter, Peck? Lose your nerve? Let 'er run!' "

And run she did; the car arrived in the center of Cleveland, at a hotel near the Public Square called the Hollenden House, in two hours and twenty-odd minutes, having averaged *fifty-five miles an hour* for the 121 miles, towns and all.

At such speeds, with only a single track just where the cars went fastest, it is not surprising that dispatching was an important function and that an elaborate ritual attended the checking and rechecking of schedules and train orders. At intervals along the single track there were sidings, turnoffs where a car could get off the main line so that one coming in the opposite direction could pass. Each siding had a telephone, from which the motorman or conductor could call in to the dispatcher. Every employee having anything to do with the cars had at frequent intervals to have his watch inspected and certified, attesting that it did not run more than thirty seconds off each week. The motorman and conductor of each train, before starting a run, called in to the dispatcher to compare the time on his watch with that on the official clock; if the watch was off he must note the variation but not adjust the watch, and if it was off thirty seconds a week it must be taken in for adjustment. Similarly, the train crews compared their watches before starting each trip and at least every three hours thereafter, all day.

The motorman of a regularly scheduled train received written orders each day, telling him at what times and at what places he was to meet cars going in the opposite direction. In addition, he had to check with the dispatcher by phone at every siding; changes were often made in the schedule because one or another car had been delayed, extras or second sections had been put on, or some emergency had occurred, and it was vital that the men on the cars know this. If a motorman was late (perhaps he had been delayed by the drawbridge at Lorain, a bridge that was a convenient alibi for passengers who suddenly got a terrible thirst on the way home) the dispatcher would "set him back a switch"—that is, change the meeting places previously arranged. If all the cars involved were running on time, the dispatcher would give a motorman clearance to proceed as scheduled to the next siding. According to the rule book of the Northern Ohio Traction & Light Company: "The dispatcher will repeat after the conductor or motorman his train and location, and will then give orders, spelling and pronouncing each meeting or passing point. The one receiving the order will write it plainly and without unauthorized abbreviation on the blank provided for that purpose, with sufficient carbon copies. He will thereupon sign his name. The one who has not taken the order will then read the order to the dispatcher, spelling as well as pronouncing each meeting or passing point, and give the time as shown by his watch and his name to the dispatcher, and if correct, the dispatcher will then give his initials and the train order number which must be repeated back to the dispatcher by the one then at the telephone. If correct, the dispatcher will say, 'Complete at . . .' giving the time, which completes the order, putting it into full force and effect. If for any reason the dispatcher does not 'Complete' an order, it is of no effect and must then be treated as though it had not been given."

If there was any doubt, they were to ask the dispatcher. "In no case," say the rules, "shall any of them attempt to influence the decision of the others as to the meaning of a train order."

Elaborate as the ritual was, it was far from foolproof, and although the interurbans were safe enough compared to automobiles, there are in their history some serious wrecks. Many of the lines did not have automatic signaling, and only gradually did they adopt various safety devices: block signaling, nonelectric rear lights (so that in a power failure the warning lantern would still burn), and a device called an anti-climber. This last was a corrugated piece of metal riveted to the sill of the car in front and back. Its purpose was to mesh with the other

Pacific Electric Motion Pictures—Improper Protection of Passenger Train, by Night

Pacific Electric Motion Pictures—Proper Position of Conductor with Superior Train Entering Siding

Pacific Electric Motion Pictures—Careless Flagging at Railroad Crossing

Pacific Electric Motion Pictures—Result of Careless Flagging at Crossing

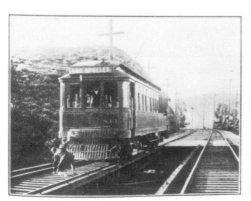

Pacific Electric Motion Pictures—Car Rounding Curve at High Speed Not Under Control, Strikes Trespasser on Narrow Bridge

Pacific Electric Motion Pictures—Car After Rounding Curve Under Control, Stops Before Reaching Bridge and Motorman Calls Attention of Trespasser to Sign

From *Electric Railway Journal*, April 4, 1914. Courtesy of Interurban Films.

car's anti-climber in a collision and thus absorb the impact. Even in high-speed collisions, the anti-climber prevented the rear car from wedging into the front one and overriding the floor. (In one accident, where anti-climbers either were not used or were not effective, a man was trapped between the floors of the two cars. When finally liberated, he was discovered to have escaped with a few bruises, but not everyone involved in such an accident was as lucky.)

"They tried for years," an ex-Cleveland, Painesville & Ashtabula conductor named Al Miller told me, "to find a way that one car can pass another on the same track. They were never able to do it, though."

Interurban accidents were almost invariably the result of human error; trainmen would disregard or misunderstand train orders; a dispatcher would take more for granted than he should have; there would be some mistake in sending or interpreting signals. The worst interurban disaster of all, a head-on collision in Kingsland, Indiana, in 1910, took place because the offending crew decided to make for two sidings beyond the one where they were supposed to meet an oncoming train. Forty-one people lost their lives and many others were seriously injured.

On Memorial Day in 1907 a wreck on the Cleveland, Southwestern killed seven people, deprived eight of one or more of their limbs, and badly crippled two others. All this because the motorman of the second section of a holiday train caught sight of a dead dog lying near the track and for some reason decided to leave his controller to get a better look at it. When a passenger called his attention to the loaded car just ahead, it was too late to stop. After his car, its front six inches higher than the rear platform of the one ahead, had sheared into the first section, the offending motorman leaped from the car and ran away. The police caught up with him the next day, saved him from a lynch mob, and took him in. He was charged with manslaughter, but suffered a mental breakdown before the trial, and finished his life in an institution, where, many contemporary observers thought, he should have been incarcerated before the wreck.

No one knows how many smaller accidents were caused by the same sort of carelessness. In the early days of the industry, when there was not much other traffic, there were some one-man cars; the motorman let the car run on by itself while he collected fares. Of course, it was not always easy to interpret signals correctly, or to know that you were misinterpreting them. Charles Peters lost a friend, who was killed, along with his young son and a third person, while riding as a passenger in a two-section trolley running between Akron and Ravenna. The first motorman stopped at a siding to call in to his dispatcher. He didn't pull the car in quite far enough and the rear end stuck out onto the main track. The motorman of the second section blew a double blast on his whistle, signaling car #1 to move in. Instead, for some reason, the first man interpreted this as orders to meet at the next switch. He shot out onto the main track, hitting the other car and killing the three passengers.

On the Meriden (Connecticut) Electric Railway in June of 1902, Conductor William Lajoie and Motorman Clarence Marvin had a fist fight over who should have first chance to read the newspaper. "The car ran wild," says a contemporary news story, "for nearly a mile, with the passengers ready to jump, but before it crashed into another car approaching, Motorman Marvin regained his senses and stopped the car. Both were fired by the company." Marvin had Lajoie arrested, but there is no record of how the case was disposed of. The NOTL rule book states that the reading of newspapers, letters, or other matter on duty, except to consult orders, rules, or timetables, is prohibited.

How serious an accident called a "split switch" could be was often determined by whether the conductor involved was more or less conscientious. When the car approached a facing switch, the conductor was supposed to get out and stand on the ground watching the wheels as they cleared the switchpoint. Sometimes a jar from a worn wheel or some other eccentricity of motion would throw the switch in the other direction after the front wheels had passed. Consequently, the front wheels would be running in one direction while the rear would be trying to go down the other track. If this happened, the conductor was to blow his whistle immediately, so that the motorman would stop before the car derailed. A lazy conductor knew that it was usually possible to watch without leaving the car step and still signal the motorman in time. Occasionally, he didn't manage it. The wheels nudged the switch over in midpassage, and the train left the track and slammed into whatever was standing nearby.

When trolley cars hit one another, both were damaged; when they hit anything else, the damage was usually one-sided. Although lighter cars were built as time went on, a certain minimum weight was necessary so they would hold the track at high speeds ("and even then

This "Be careful" poster was put out by the Interstate Public Service Company in or around 1924. An earlier poster was published, which showed an actual crash, but was withdrawn as being too gory. Reproduced by Vane A. Jones. © Reprinted 1975 by Traction and Models.

they'd swing and sway with Sammy Kaye," Mr. Platt said. He invited me to go outside right then and there and look along the New York Central track that ran near his home in Sandusky. "That's supposed to be a first-class railroad, and you'll see how the track dips at the joints. It's hard to maintain track.") The weight of an interurban car varied from about forty to about seventy tons. Today's automobiles would be nowhere near their class, of course, and the autos of the early 1900s

were far lighter (if not flimsier). This, combined with the fact that they seemed to have been all over the tracks, made for a rather destructive relationship—one that had sometimes tragic and sometimes comic results.

For some reason the man behind the wheel of a Model T acquired prophetic vision; his only mistake was to apply the prophecy to the present time. He felt that his mastery of the motorcar was enough to make the interurbans disappear, and although of course eventually it did, many drivers acted as though it had already happened. The fantasy afflicted even trainmen: an off-duty conductor, driving alongside the track and waving gaily at his friends in the crew then swung across the track in front of the trolley car as though his occupation was already obsolete.

The most bizarre combination of events of this sort, however, was visited upon Homer Frederick, who served from 1912 to 1932 on the Akron-Cleveland line, first as conductor and then "on the front end." One July 4 in the twenties, dead-heading along at sixty or sixty-five miles an hour on a right-of-way beside a main road, Mr. Frederick saw, to his dismay and astonishment, a little Ford pull off the road and stop on the track ahead of him. It was too late to avoid hitting the automobile, but by putting the trolley car into reverse and slamming on the brakes, Mr. Frederick managed to modify the impact somewhat. He and the conductor got out and found, first, two women in the front seat, hurt but by no means dead. They then traced the sound of childish screams to the automobile's rumble seat. This was closed, whether as a result of the crash or before it Mr. Frederick did not know. In it were two children and three or four chickens, all highly vocal but unhurt. The next, and most horrifying, sight of all was that of a man with no legs lying in the road. There was an unaccountable absence of blood, and the man seemed otherwise unhurt and in reasonably good spirits, if unjustifiably angry at the trolleymen. Mr. Frederick and his conductor then realized that it was sometime in the past that the man had lost his legs; the Ford was specially equipped to be hand driven.

Why he had turned onto the track and stopped, no one ever really found out. Not even, Mr. Frederick told me roguishly, when four years later the same man, in the same car, pulled across the track down which Mr. Frederick was barreling in his trolley car, swung around, and hit the interurban broadside.

This second mishap led to court action. There one of the witnesses for the motorist was a young man who turned up in Mr. Frederick's life years later, when the interurban was gone and Mr. Frederick was an instructor for the Cleveland Transit System. During a coffee break, the unknowing young man, whom Mr. Frederick was breaking in as a motorman, told his instructor about the time he had testified in a trolley v. motorcar case. Mr. Frederick was gratified to hear him say, "I was wrong. I said the motorman could have stopped, but now that I know something about running a trolley car, I can see that he couldn't have." "I never let on," Mr. Frederick said.

"You hear about the brave engineer sticking to his post in an accident," Ed Wilcox told me, talking about wild, if less than tragic, accidents he had known. "The only reason he sticks to his post so brave is because he's too scared to run!" During his thirty years on electric railroads, Mr. Wilcox hit a number of vehicles that didn't belong on his rails; typical was an asphalt truck which damaged no more than the Sunday dresses of a group of Oberlin College girls riding the trolley to a concert. "Warm asphalt all over everything," exclaimed Mr. Wilcox with more amusement than dismay. "I was pretty near back to the smoker time she hit!" (The truck driver, after backing onto the track, had jumped out of the cab and run, too.)

Animals on the track, although frequent, were a nuisance rather than a threat. Unless the trolley company had undertaken to fence the right-of-way, the dead cow or horse was their responsibility and they paid for it. Often, although the term "public relations" had probably not yet been coined, the company paid for damaged animals even when they were not legally liable. Less than scrupulous farmers took advantage of this. When Mr. Platt's trolley hit a cow one night, he knew the route well enough to realize that there was only one farm to which the animal could have belonged. He and his motorman stopped the car (passengers, it appears, took such postponements of their trip as casually as they were made, and most often welcomed the diversion), and walked back a half mile or so to the farmhouse.

"I'm afraid we killed a cow of yours," Mr. Platt said to the farmer.

"That's the best cow I had!" cried the bereaved husbandman.

"Here you sit," said Mr. Platt, leading in like Perry Mason, "half a mile from the track. How'd you know which one we killed?"

On another night, the bag was a horse. This time Mr. Platt had noticed a light in a barn they'd passed a minute or two before. "Let's go see why they've got a light in the barn at 9:42 at night," he said to the motorman with an appropriate chronological accuracy. They hiked back to the barn, where they found two men on whom Mr. Platt decided to try shock tactics. "Why'd you tie that horse on the track?" he demanded. "I hit the nail on the head so exactly," he says now, "that they confessed. The old nag wasn't good for anything. They figured they'd see what they could get from the Lake Shore Electric for him."

Owls were a bother, pheasants a minor danger. A low-flying pheasant could, and often did, break a trolley car's windshield.

The public called it a "cowcatcher." Trolley fans say it's a "safety fender" or a "pilot." It came in a variety of shapes and sizes and scooped up a variety of wild (and not so wild) life. Photograph courtesy of Frances G. Scott.

Occasionally, people were hit, most often by accident, although one old lady bent on suicide threw herself onto the track three or four times before she finally achieved it. The car tossed her seventy-five feet through the air and knocked off her high button shoes without opening one button.

The safety fender, "pilot," or "life guard" on the front of some trolley cars gathered up light buggies, small boys daring one another to run in front of the car, and other foreign objects on the track. The effectiveness of the fender (as of all safety devices) was in inverse ratio to the speed of the car. That is why, when Motorman William Lang, running his Lake Shore Electric trolley at fifty-five miles an hour, saw with horror two-year-old Leila Smith playing on the track in front of him, he did not put his trust in the life guard. Setting the controls in reverse, Lang climbed out on the fender and scooped up the child as the train came up to her. For this act of heroism, Mr. Lang received a Carnegie Medal, an Interstate Commerce Commission award authorized by President Theodore Roosevelt, and a bad back that necessitates his wearing a brace to this day.

Trolley men, like roentgenologists and plumbers, game wardens, and short-order cooks, were of all sorts, from irresponsible fools, such as the crew who tried to jump two sidings ahead at Kingsland, to brave and conscientious men like William Lang. The ones I have met were, inevitably, elderly. (Mr. Platt is head of the Lake Shore Electric Pioneers Association, and as he ruefully pointed out to me, "We don't get any new members.") Most of them are now retired, although one of the youngest, Martin Ackerman, who began working for the Lake Shore Electric in 1926, was still a motorman/conductor on the Cleveland "Rapid," that city's mass transit line, when I met him a few years ago. Others work part-time as school crossing guards; one is a night clerk in a Cleveland motel; an eighty-four-year-old former motorman on the Cleveland, Painesville & Ashtabula now sells real estate in the towns he used to serve on the trolley.

Although they seemed, without exception, gentle and gentlemanly men, there were continual hints in their conversation, their demeanor, and in such sources as the company rule books, that working the interurbans was more of a frontiersman's job than a desk man's. At a reunion dinner of the Cleveland, Painesville & Ashtabula that I attended, the chairman called upon one of the members to offer grace. A short bouncy man in his seventies sitting next to me snorted, "Asking a trolley man to offer a prayer!"

A man like Ed Wilcox, who has so much energy and spirit at eighty-nine, was by his own admission a rough man to cross when he was riding the cars. Drunks pulled knives on him and had to be cowed with a .32 applied to the ribs. (The gun was not official issue, but Mr. Wilcox found it handy.) A huge ex-wrestler once boarded his car and flatly refused to pay his fare. When a passenger does not pay his fare, say the rule books, he may be ejected from the car, at the next regular stop, "using only such force as is sufficient to expel the offending passenger, with a reasonable regard for his personal safety, without the use of harsh language or display of ill temper." Apparently this does not work with liquored-up former wrestlers. Mr. Wilcox got the fare by waving his leather-covered billy in the passenger's face. When the disgruntled wrestler left the trolley car at his destination, he directed some "harsh language" at the much smaller and slighter Mr. Wilcox. That gentleman, realizing that he held a strategic position—on the car step, above the wrestler—jumped down swinging and broke the fellow's nose.

On his way to court the next day (in a trolley car, of course) to answer for this Mr. Wilcox met his superintendent, who, hearing about the incident, decided to come along as a character witness. "Do you hire a man on his ability to fight?" the judge asked him.

"No, your honor," said the superintendent, "but sometimes it comes in handy."

The second basis for an ejectment, says the rule book, is disorderly or offensive conduct, and when such an ejectment is made, the conductor must tender to the ejectee the unused portion of his fare.

The trainmen were to remember that they were "engaged in a public service, in which they are constantly called upon to exercise great patience, forbearance and self-control. . . . Boisterous or profane language on or about the premises is prohibited, as are intoxicants before reporting for duty or while on duty. Employees known to be addicted to their use, or to frequent saloons or places of low resort, will not be retained by the service."

"Frequenting saloons," however, was a practice so widespread that the companies could not afford to enforce its prohibition, and the evidence shows that trolley men were not fired for drinking until it became drunkenness. If they had been fired, most of the lines would have had to close down for want of personnel.

Mr. Wilcox had reminded his superintendent of a similar fact of trolley life when he was ordered to ride the cars at night to check on a report that conductors were "carrying on" in the cars with girls. The job was distasteful, but Wilcox halfheartedly pursued it for a few evenings, after which it came time for his report. "Well?" the superintendent demanded. "Are they carrying on with girls?" "If I tell you they are," replied Ed, "who the hell will you get to run the cars?"

Genuine crime on the interurbans doesn't seem to have been a particularly profitable sort. In 1922 a latter-day Jesse James got $250 from the passengers and crew of a trolley car near Columbus. He had boarded the train in that city and conscientiously paid his fare to Hibernia, a village on the line. However, at the first crossing he rang the bell to get off; instead of doing so, he put a gun in the motorman's ribs and relieved him of the cashbox and the passengers of their valuables. Perhaps the dollar was worth more in 1908; in October of that year a holdup man got away with a mere $21 on an interurban car, after threatening the conductor's life. As a result, the company armed every motorman and conductor on the line.

Not only outsiders robbed the interurbans. "What is your name?" an ancient trolley joke has the superintendent asking the applicant for a conductor's job. "Rob Nichols," answers the jobseeker. "We can't hire you!" cries the super. "We've got too many men called that already!" Motive, means, and opportunity made it easy for a conductor to pocket his own fringe benefits; some of them got very inventive about outsmarting the company's inspectors. Management installed Ohmer registers to keep the conductors in line. These clocklike devices, which former trolley riders will remember, were placed in a high and conspicuous place in the car. The conductor had to ring the Ohmer register once for each fare he collected by pulling a cord hanging from it. The cord rang a bell and the hands of the dial advanced. In fact, any conductor worth his brass buttons could ring up a pocketful of fares so rapidly that a company spy would have hopelessly lost count by the time the last fare was (or was not) entered. The conductor added to the illusion by ringing a bell he carried in his pocket each time he feigned a pull on the cord.

Interurban pay was never so high as to make a trolley man sneer at temptation. In 1912, when Mr. Peters started on the miners' line in Dubois, he was paid sixteen cents an hour. If he worked out satisfactorily, the rate went up a penny every six months until it reached nineteen cents; that was the top. Rates in 1903 on the Cleveland, Painesville & Ashtabula were sixteen cents, eighteen cents, and twenty cents. The larger lines paid more, of course, but even their pay rates were hardly handsome: they varied from about thirty cents to fifty cents an hour during the most successful interurban period. There was no overtime pay and there were no days off. Beginners were on the "extra board," substituting for absent trainmen or running extra cars. "Front-of-the-car" men (motormen) and "back-of-the-car" men (conductors) got the same pay rates. A dispatcher's job carried more pay per hour, but in practice the trainmen could make more money since they almost always worked longer hours. Ward Platt once figured out that he worked 3,650 hours and 50 minutes in one year, an average of 10 hours a day, every single day of the year. Jobs were seven-days-a-week, fifty-two-weeks-a-year arrangements. It was possible to get time off (unpaid, of course) only at the pleasure of the supervisor.

Penalties for minor accidents or infractions of the rules were usually suspensions, and they were not light. One motorman pulled three freight cars through the streets of Cleveland to the freight depot in the center of the city in violation of city rules limiting him to two cars. He got there without attracting the attention of anyone who cared, but the dispatcher at the depot was moved to report him and he was suspended for thirty days. The men tried hard to organize into a union, but the years of the interurbans were in general antiunion years, and organization wasn't very effective until near the end of the industry's life.

The conductor was, at least nominally, the boss of the train, and since the motorman spent all his working time operating the car, a variety of continual but not continuous responsibilities fell upon the conductor. He collected fares or sold tickets, answered questions, kept order in the car, and usually made schedule checks with the dispatcher which the motorman corroborated. When the trolley wire was down, for whatever reason, it was the conductor's job to pick it up off the track. "You tie it up and then creep under it," one man said. For this trick, he used any makeshift tool that didn't conduct electricity, most often the motorman's wooden stool. Sometimes he tied a rope to a stick and maneuvered the wire off the track with that; there was also a ready-made version of this called a "come along." It was the conductor, also, who pulled down one trolley at the end of the line and connected the other, preparatory to running back the other way. On a single-trolley car, he had to pull down the trolley and swing it around to the other direction. Running a car against the trolley could pull down the power line.

When the trolley was "lost"—came off the wire—for any reason (usually because the motorman took a curve too fast), the conductor put it back again. Replacing the trolley exposed conductors to an occupational hazard known as "trolley flash." If the motorman didn't shut off the air compressors that pumped air for the brakes (and he never did), when the conductor was fiddling with the trolley, electricity would arc from the wire to the trolley wheel and tiny bits of copper would shower down. Often, one of these slivers of copper would lodge in the conductor's eyeball. "At the time you didn't feel it," Martin Ackerman said, "and you'd work for four or five hours, but when you went home to bed that night and shut your eyes, you would feel the whole inside of your head burn. The only thing to do then was go to the doctor the next morning. He would anesthetize your eye and take out the piece of copper imbedded in your eyeball with a tiny knife." In his eleven years as conductor on the Lake Shore Electric, Mr. Ackerman said, this had happened to him four or five times, but he knew a conductor named Hawkins whose glasses were so pock-marked with bits of copper that he had to peer around them to read; it was Mr. Ackerman's belief that he wore them solely as protection for his eyes.

The two-man crew of a car in Ashtabula, one morning in 1908, climbed up on the roof to change trolley poles because one of the wheels was broken. Trolley poles are sprung, in order to put the proper pressure between the wheel and the wire, and one of the technical bones of contention was just what was the optimum pressure that would maximize contact and minimize wear on the wheel. The pole these trainmen were pulling down got away from them, whirled around and knocked the conductor off the roof, giving him "a painful foot bruise," while the motorman grabbed the trolley wire to keep from falling and received a 500-volt charge. "Both men continued their runs, but Holt [the bruised conductor] laid off at Conneaut until that evening."

Minor occupational hazards of this nature, thumbs banged or fingers pinched when a motorman reversed an unfamiliar controller too quickly, bumps, burns, bruises were, of course, to be expected. Doubtless electric shock and burns were not rare; the rule books included instructions on first aid and artificial respiration "even when the victim appears to be dead." Bill Heinemann has a theory that electric shock will not kill a man unless it is accompanied by lethal burns. This idea may or may not be accepted by medical science, but Mr. Heinemann has an empirical basis for his theory. In August, 1904, in a power plant of the Cleveland, Southwestern & Columbus Railway, he backed into a hot wire and got a charge of 18,000 volts —about ten times the voltage used in the 100 percent effective electric chair. He attributes his undeniable survival to the fact that the charge found a short path through his body, bypassing his vital organs and leaving him with relatively minor burns.

In common with transportation men from the Phoenicians to the Astronauts, the trolley men were constantly and intimately concerned with weather. In the summer there were no real problems; the conductor had only, as his rule book instructed, to "close the windows

A rare photograph of car #188, on interurban duty out of Lewiston, Maine, in a snowstorm. This is a very light model for interurban running, and the pilot ("cowcatcher") is an unusual feature. Photograph from the collection of G. J. Sas, Fairfield Models.

immediately at the beginning of a rain storm, without waiting to see if it is a severe one or not." Of course, lightning storms sometimes knocked out the power, but that was all in a day's riding.

If lightning struck a car, through the trolley, the car was well enough grounded so the people on it did not get hurt. What it would do was burn out the motor; the charge went through too fast to trip the circuit breakers. But there was no danger.

Mr. Peters told me that most trolley men welcomed the rain. "It seemed to make a better contact between the trolley and the wire," he said. The electrics coped with occasional sections of flooded track by running cars shuttle fashion to either side of the flood and ferrying the passengers across between them in rowboats.

None of the men I have met look back on snow with much excitement, either, which is surprising in this lake area, where eight or twelve inches can fall several times a winter, and where storms sometimes pile drifts six feet high or more. Every trolley line had one or more snowplows. Since snowplows ran when there were no other cars on the line, they could use more voltage; the entire output of the power plant was theirs. However, the Cleveland, Southwestern once bought a snowplow that took too much power for their lines; it was never used and was finally left to deteriorate in a barn. Even the ordinary snowplows had a way of lifting the planks in a crossing, packing snow under them, and eventually dislodging the rails. But they did their job—did it well enough, indeed, for the interurban track often to be the only cleared ground in the area; more than once trucks were hit by interurban cars as they brazenly took to the trolley track because the roads were impassable.

Several times a winter cars got derailed, and sometimes stuck, on snowy track. On a Sunday Ed Wilcox abandoned a car stuck in the snow and it was not dug out until the following Wednesday. Mr. Peters remembers a storm "along about in 1912" that stranded a car full of passengers at a crossroads about twenty miles east of Cleveland. Fortunately, the owner of a small farm nearby took in the whole mob, killed a cow to feed them for three days, and later received $900 from the company for his hospitality. Although most trolley cars were provided with windshield wipers, in a bad storm the motorman was compelled to ride with his head out the window, peering through the whirling flakes at the track ahead.

It was in the spring and fall that the weather was touchiest, as far as the interurban men were concerned, because it is in those seasons that

Fighting snow on line in front of the dispatcher's office. Philadelphia Suburban Transit car. Photograph courtesy of 35 Slides, Colorado Springs, Colorado.

this area sees frequent sleet storms. Sleet on the trolley wire would cause the trolley wheel to jump on and off, making and breaking the connection. Mr. Platt told me that in a bad sleet storm you could see the resultant arcs of electricity flash bright blue ("electric blue") from as far as twenty miles away. The cars carried sand to blow onto slippery tracks, but there wasn't a lot they could do about ice on the trolley wire.

Leon George, an ex-freight conductor on the ABC, described to me a device called a "sleet cutter," which was supposed to scrape the ice off the wire. It was a copper shoe that fitted over or replaced the trolley wheel; at the top was a blade that ran along the wire dislodging the ice. But it was not wholly satisfactory; since it couldn't eliminate the arcing completely, the shoe itself would soon burn out. I assumed that "soon" meant "in a few trips," until Mr. George mentioned that they customarily used six shoes in the thirty miles between Cleveland and Cuyahoga Falls. He had reason to be skeptical about them; he remembers the night he covered that thirty miles in a sleet storm, sitting on top of the ice-covered car, straddling the clerestory roof, and knocking sleet off the trolley wire with a brake club.

Two styles of the scrapers the interurbans optimistically used to scrape sleet and ice from the trolley wire. The scraper was attached to the trolley wheel or shoe. Illustrations from *The Electric Railway Dictionary*, courtesy of Newton K. Gregg.

The weight of ice on the wire often pulled it down, and a catenary wire—a wire suspended between two sets of poles on "messenger" wires connecting the poles—could be pulled down in three-mile sections by an accumulation of sleet. (Down wires, like stuck drawbridges, were the stuff of husbands' alibis, and there were far more down wires reported to wives than to dispatchers.)

6
Three Long Rides

The enormous number of interurban lines built (or begun) during the two interurban building booms makes it impossible to try to describe many in detail. But three different lines—the West Penn Railways near Pittsburgh, the Illinois Terminal Railroad in the Midwest, and the Pacific Electric in Southern California—deserve a more detailed look, since together they provide a varied sampling of interurban trolley service in the United States.

The Illinois Terminal, large, successful, freight-interchanging, midwestern, heavy; the Pacific Electric, longest of any that could be called "interurban"; the oddball West Penn, a particularly idiosyncratic local service—all were successful over a long period of time. So many of the nation's 700 lines died in infancy, so many others lived through a sickly childhood to succumb in their early twenties, that these three might be called atypical because parts of each, at least, were in existence for fifty years or more.

The Illinois Terminal Railroad is the favorite of many railfans, and is certainly an interurban line that typifies solidity and, in a certain context, success. Originally the Illinois Traction Company, the ITR began as a typical midwestern line, running in Central Illinois and into St. Louis, Missouri. Several fortunate circumstances—plus skillful management—combined to account for its longevity, although even so there were gaps in the proposed main lines that were not closed during the entire life of the line.

In 1903, the first track of the Illinois Terminal Railroad was laid—a 35-mile line from Champaign to Danville, Illinois. As early as 1909 more than a hundred trains a day were running out of Springfield. By the late 1940s, the line included 400 miles of track, and served St. Louis, Peoria, Decatur, and many other cities in the south-central part of the state. The completed system consisted of three lines: 172 miles, from St. Louis to Peoria via Carlinville and Springfield; 123 miles from Springfield east through Decatur and Champaign to Danville; and 66 miles north from Decatur through Clinton and Bloomington to a junction with the main line Decatur-Peoria trains at Mackinaw. There was limited service, with parlor and dining cars, between Peoria and St. Louis, and suburban and street railway service around St. Louis and in the cities served.

Early Illinois Terminal cars were typical wood interurbans, but in an effort to look up-to-date, the line in the twenties and thirties rebuilt its equipment by attaching steel plates to the outside, covering the stained glass, and coming up with a car that looked like the more modern all-metal ones. The Illinois Terminal cars, thus remodeled, along with heavy steel ones built from scratch, were originally painted traction orange, the traditional streetcar color, and had distinctive arched windows that are a joy to many a trolley car modeler.

Illinois Terminal passenger equipment was the most luxurious in the industry, and the line had a predominance of parlor cars, always synonymous with elegance on steam or trolley lines. The furnishings varied, but a common feature was the wicker furniture—armchairs with upholstered seats—and the elaborate tulip-shaped glass lampshades that hung from the polished ceiling. In 1948 the company ordered new cars, streamlined "electroliners" (whose diners served "electrosteaks" and "electroburgers"). These were the last interurban cars ever built.

Illinois Terminal was one of the only three interurbans that ran sleeping cars. In 1907 convertible parlor/sleeping cars (named *Theodore* and *Francis*) were purchased from the bankrupt Holland Palace Car Company. The company had been founded by an entrepreneur named Harris P. Holland, who had hoped his cars would become the "Pullmans" of the interurbans. The sleepers went into night operation between East St. Louis, Springfield, and Decatur, leaving at midnight and arriving in Decatur at 9:30 the next morning,

"The Owl"

By Night

"Capitol Limited"

By Day

Sleeping Car Train

EXTRA LONG BERTHS,
WINDOWS IN UPPERS,
NO SMOKE, NO CINDERS

Parlor Car Train

EASY PARLOR CHAIRS, LIBRARY,
OBSERVATION PLATFORM,
MEALS A LA CARTE

Lv. St. Louis.....................11:45 P.M.	
*Ar. Springfield.................... 4:05 A.M.	
Ar. Peoria........................ 6:35 A.M.	
*Sleeper set out at Springfield	

Lv. St. Louis......................11:45 P.M.
*Ar. Springfield.................... 4:05 A.M.
Ar. Peoria........................ 6:35 A.M.
*Sleeper set out at Springfield
Lv. Peoria........................11:45 P.M.
Lv. Springfield.................... 2:25 A.M.
Ar. St. Louis.................... 6:45 A.M.

Lv. St. Louis......................4:00 P.M.
Lv. Springfield....................7:30 P.M.
Ar. Peoria........................9:50 P.M.

Lv. Peoria........................4:00 P.M.
Lv. Springfield....................6:20 P.M.
Ar. St. Louis......................9:50 P.M.

"THE ILLINI"—SLEEPING CAR—EVERY OTHER NIGHT BETWEEN ST. LOUIS and CHAMPAIGN

Timetables advertised their lines, and the Illinois Terminal Company's had more to offer than most.

after lying over for four hours in Springfield so as to end the trip at a reasonable hour.

Fare for the berth to either city, above the rail fare, was one dollar. With dreams of eventually having sleeper service from St. Louis to Chicago, the ITR ordered more sleeping cars built to its own specifications. They ran for many years in the central Illinois–St. Louis area, although, because the connection with Chicago was never made, the original purpose was never fulfilled. In fact, most of the time the cars were run as straight parlor cars.

The largest single investment any interurban company made was the bridge the Illinois Terminal built over the Mississippi at Venice, Illinois, near St. Louis. "The Mississippi is a formidable body of water

CONDENSED SCHEDULES OF THROUGH SERVICE

*11 55	*7 10	*4 30	*1 00	*10 00	*7 10	*4 30				9 35	11 45	2 53	5 45	8 55	12 15	6 20
2 15	8 55	6 10	2 50	11 40	8 51	6 30	Ar.	Carlinville	Lv.	7 49	9 59	1 12	4 06	7 12	10 35	4 01
3 41	10 00	7 13	3 55	12 44	9 58	7 43	Ar.	Springfield	Lv.	6 35	8 49	12 04	2 57	6 05	9 24	2 25
4 46	10 53	7 54	4 37	1 25		8 30	Ar.	Lincoln	Lv.		8 10	11 20	2 18	5 24	8 41	1 19
6 35	1 15	10 10	6 40	3 25	12 30	9 55	Ar.	Bloomington	Lv.		6 55	8 35	12 30	3 35	6 30	10 45
6 05	12 05	9 00	5 45	2 30		9 45	Ar.	Peoria	Lv.		7 10	10 15	1 10	4 20	7 30	11 58
7 54		8 30	5 05	2 20	11 05		Ar.	Decatur	Lv.	3 10	7 28	9 50	1 50	4 55	8 07	
8 45		9 18	5 53	3 10	11 53		Ar.	Monticello	Lv.	2 19	6 35	8 56	12 55	4 04	7 16	
9 23		9 55	6 30	3 50	12 30		Ar.	Champaign	Lv.	*1 45	*6 00	8 15	12 18	3 28	6 40	9 10
9 31			6 38	3 58	12 38		Ar.	Urbana	Lv.			8 03	12 08	3 18	6 29	8 59
10 30			7 35	4 55	1 35		Ar.	Danville	Lv.			*7 05	*11 10	*2 20	*5 30	*8 00

* Daily.   Light face figures indicate A. M.   **Dark face figures indicate P. M.**

at St. Louis town," writes Dr. Rea F. Chittenden, the source of a wealth of both railroad and traction information. "A *big* steel bridge just for 'trolley lines' was a rarity."

The bridge, including its approaches, was nearly half a mile long and rose to fifty feet over mean high water. In fact, it was because the

 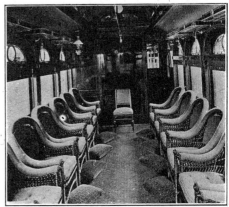

Can this be a *trolley?* Interior and exterior of a 1911 café car, Aurora, Elgin & Chicago Railroad. Illustration from *The Electric Railway Dictionary,* courtesy of Newton K. Gregg.

company's funds were so drained after spending three million dollars on the bridge that William B. McKinley, the line's first owner, was never able to build as he had planned from Streator, Illinois to Mackinaw Junction, which would have linked St. Louis, through the Chicago, Ottawa & Peoria, which he controlled, to Chicago.

The happy combination of circumstances contributing to the longevity of the Illinois Terminal were: the absense of steam road passenger competition on the line's major runs; its high-speed en-

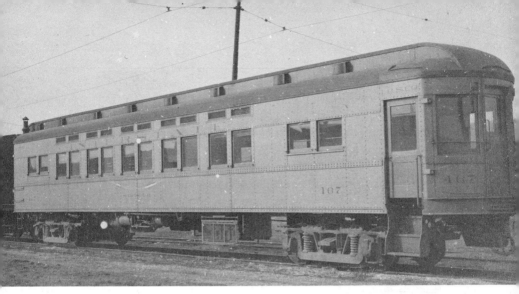

An Interstate Public Service Company sleeping car. Interurban sleepers, unlike those on the steam road, had upper-berth windows, perhaps because there was no problem about cinders from the locomotive. Photograph by Glenn Nicely, courtesy of Blair Foulds.

trance into downtown St. Louis; the poor steam road service to Peoria from the south; the industrial freight traffic in the line's local area—traffic of a kind particularly well suited for trolleys—as well as coal and grain; and a variety of freight traffic not threatened by competition from trucks. The most important element in the Illinois Terminal's enviable prosperity, however, was its managers' acuity in realizing early how important carload freight was to revenue, and in acting aggressively on that realization to seek interchange business with the steam roads. When profits from passenger service were low, the freight business came to the rescue.

The freight business was diverse; the line carried coal, gasoline, grain, and a variety of manufactured goods. Besides standard freight cars, the line owned ice-cooled refrigerator cars suited for interchange. It served mines, brick works, and gave exclusive service to a major washed-gravel plant. It used heavy articulated electric locomotives that were as powerful as any on an interurban line.

To speed up its freight operation, the ITR built belt lines around some of the major cities it served. This did away with slow running in the city. Passengers weren't happy about it—they were forced to find transportation from the outskirts (a complaint we now associate with air travelers), but the freight *and* passenger schedules were speeded enormously thereby.

In building freight interchange business the ITR found resistance. The steam roads were not anxious to make life easy for their competitors, even if the concession was to their own advantage. Local Chambers of Commerce, whose communities were served by the interurban, helped twist arms for the good of the line. They had their reasons—they were out to develop highly taxable industrial sites on the periphery of their towns.

Equipment was another obstacle to interchange. Interurban cars were built with radial couplers to attach the cars together. The radial is a free-moving coupler with a wide span that allowed multi-car trains to negotiate very tight curves so they could use the local trolley tracks in towns where the interurbans joined the streetcars. But the railroads would not accept radially coupled cars, and there were local laws as well as tight corners keeping cars with steam-road couplers off city

Besides passenger, freight, and maintenance-of-way cars, the Illinois Terminal Company had many special-purpose trolleys. This is an ice-cooled wooden refrigerator car (1911). Illustration from *The Electric Railway Dictionary*, courtesy of Newton K. Gregg.

The last word in interurban cars. Built in 1945, they offered the Illinois Terminal no more than a brief reprieve. Courtesy of Herbert Georg Studio, Springfield, Illinois.

tracks. The belt lines skirting cities on the Illinois Terminal's routes turned out to be a blessing for this reason.

Still another vexing problem the interurban faced in freight interchange was getting its boxcars back. Grain moved out of the Illinois Terminal area in ITR freight cars in steam road trains: very little comparable goods moved back in. As a result, ITR freight cars would go out loaded with grain and drop out of sight for months at a time.

In grim desperation, Illinois Terminal built its own grain elevator. There, the electric cars picked up the grain, then rather laboriously had to transfer it to standard boxcars on the Chicago & Eastern Illinois steam road.

After World War II, passenger traffic declined, in spite of the management's optimism in ordering the new Electroliners. Routes were dropped one by one. The freight business, however, was still viable enough so that in 1956, when all passenger service was eliminated, a group of eleven railroads bought the line. They replaced the electric locos with (smelly old!) Diesels, and added right-of-way on their own various lines to the Illinois Terminal track. Down went the trolley wire, and with it the Illinois Terminal Railroad.

This is an unpainted brass model, HO scale, of the Pacific Electric's elegant 1929 business car. Photograph by Thomas J. Ayres. Reproduced from the catalogue of E. Suydam & Co., Duarte, California, with their kind permission.

If the Illinois Terminal was, in the eyes of purists, the largest **true** interurban service, the Pacific Electric was certainly the largest that by definition could be called interurban. At the height of its existence, the Pacific Electric operated over a thousand miles of track and nearly 800 route miles.

When the various lines that formed the Pacific Electric first came into being in 1895–1905, they were typical short-distance interurban lines. As the communities around them grew and merged, the Pacific Electric took on the characteristics of a suburban rapid transit facility.

Henry Huntington, nephew of the Central Pacific's Collis P. Huntington, and himself president of the Southern Pacific, saw the Los Angeles area as a natural locale for an interurban. Being a man of action—and capital—he built one of the first lines out of Los Angeles, to Pasadena and nearby communities. It was later joined to another Huntington property, the Los Angeles Interurban Railway, which went to Glendale and Santa Ana. From that beginning, an enormous network of routes covered the Los Angeles area from San Fernando to

Balboa, and beyond San Bernardino to Arrowhead Springs, Redlands, Riverside, and Corona. Some of the lines were oddities, beginning and ending in different parts of Los Angeles, but looping out to other cities on the way.

For good measure, Huntington built himself a trolley spur to his home, so that in the morning he had only to step outside his front door and into his private car (which contained kitchen and bathroom facilities and a wood-burning fireplace) to be taken to his offices by trolley. A rather glorified version, indeed, of the Ohio farmer with an interurban stop at the edge of his alfalfa field!

The Pacific Electric was a hodgepodge of different types of cars and service, which is one reason it defies precise definition. From street trolleys to heavy freight operations, the line ran deluxe parlor car trains, a six-car boat train connecting with the Catalina Island boat, huge steel interurban cars and single truck trolleys one step removed

The Mt. Lowe cars on the Pacific Electric have the typical interurban arched windows. These are the cars that made the long climb to Rubio Canyon. Shown in a brass reproduction, before painting. Photograph reproduced from the catalogue of E. Suydam & Co., Duarte, California, with their kind permission.

from Toonerville. There was even a mile-long subway (really more of a long tunnel) and a two-block elevated section.

California's temperate weather and scenic variety lends itself to excursions, and the Pacific Electric milked that source of fares. It ran picnic excursions, sightseeing excursions, rides to mountains and the seashore. A famous tourist route was the Mount Lowe line, which carried excursionists up Rubio Canyon and to the summit of Echo Mountain by inclined railway. Here, they would find facilities for horseback riding, a museum, an observatory, even two hotels to stay in. An extension of that ride, the "Alpine Division," took the traveler through spectacular mountain scenery to Mount Lowe Springs on a roadbed carved out of solid rock. It was a favorite from 1898 to 1948. Then, nature conspired to match the economic decline of the trolley line, and hit the region with a series of disasters—fires, rock slides, windstorms, and the mortal catastrophe, a cloudburst that wiped out the line itself.

Other tours on the trolley took sightseers through the fruit country. Motion pictures reigned in Southern California during the Pacific Electric's years, and trips to view the studios and the homes of the stars were popular.

Some tours had a sterner purpose. Trackage was laid to undeveloped areas; prospects would be taken out in the trolley to inspect the site, plied with free barbecue and sales pitches, entertained by bands and other gimmicks and, it was hoped, sold a lot. The community thus created would eventually swell the passenger traffic. Hollywood was developed this way, and so were other Los Angeles area colonies.

When World War II brought servicemen, defense workers, and their families to Southern California, and gas rationing and a freeze on automobile manufacture to the entire country, the Pacific Electric found it had so many riders that it had to revive old wooden cars that had been put out to pasture and borrow cars from abandoned interurban lines in the San Francisco area.

It was a last gasp, however. The early fifties brought the Pacific Electric back to reality. The passenger business was sold to the Los Angeles Metropolitan Coach Lines, which substituted all-bus service. Henry Huntington had long before taken to riding to his offices in a chauffeur-driven limousine. The Glendale–Burbank line, begun in 1904, was abandoned in 1955.

In western Pennsylvania near Pittsburgh, a trolley line was built that was unique in many ways. Its earliest predecessor companies began running in 1889, most of the track was built in the late 1890s and early 1900s, and when the last car made its run sixty-three years later, it left behind, not unheeding commuters in their gasoline buses and automobiles, but a bereft and mourning populace.

The West Penn Railways must have been created by a most rugged individualist—one of those people who disdain store-bought gadgets and rig up perfectly satisfactory mechanisms out of old bobby pins, chewing gum, and empty cellophane-tape spools.

The line owned 339 miles of trackage in three states, and most of it was built on the oddball Pennsylvania Trolley gauge of 5′ 2½″, instead of the standard 4′ 8½″ gauge of most railroads and trolley lines. The gauge matched the street railways in Pittsburgh, and had been adopted by that city to keep the standard-gauge Pennsylvania Railroad trains from invading the city streets.

The West Penn company operated six different routes around Pittsburgh and in nearby West Virginia, and if you add its connection (which was corporate but not physical) with the Hagerstown & Frederick in Maryland, it was one of the rare systems that had

Old and new in brief coexistence. The Pacific Electric's Big Red Cars and the Metropolitan Transport Authority's buses that replaced them. Photograph courtesy of Leo Caloia, Audio Visual Designs.

trackage in three different states. It went through the beautiful but difficult hill country of western Pennsylvania and eastern West Virginia.

Herman Rinke, former railroad man who was in charge of the signal tower in Grand Central Terminal, and has for many years been active in the Electric Railroaders' Association, told me about the West Penn's amazing signal system.

Most interurban lines ran on single track and had more or less elaborate electrical signaling systems to keep the cars from crashing into one another. The signals were automatic and based on one car's setting off a string of electrical impulses that triggered visual signals for both an oncoming car and one following behind. The West Penn, on the other hand, depended trustingly on a simple series of 40-watt light bulbs, crudely but effectively protected from rain, snow, and bird droppings by small wooden canopies. These light bulbs were placed along the track on every third power pole.

At the passing sidings—the extra bit of track that allowed a car to

Everything about the West Penn Railway was unusual. Although two other trolley lines had somewhat similar cars, this West Penn 700 series was not quite the same. The dropped center door may look clumsy, but it was a boon to women passengers in hobble skirts. Photograph courtesy of G. J. Sas, Fairfield Models.

Open cars weren't always confined to cities. Here is the West Penn version of the glorious "summer trolleys" that let in the breezes it stirred up. Photograph courtesy of 35 Slides, Colorado Springs, Colorado.

get off the main line—there was a pair of switches. When a car went into a siding, the motorman leaned out of his front door and threw both switches. One of them lit the bulbs on his right in the section of track he was about to traverse. The other turned off the bulbs on his right in the section he had just left.

If, when he arrived at a siding and saw that a bulb on his left was lit, the motorman knew a car was approaching on the single track in the other direction. (That bulb would be on the approaching motorman's right; it hadn't been turned off yet, so the car was still on its way.) The first motorman, therefore, had to wait at the siding for the approaching car to pass.

If the light on his right, past the siding, was burning, he could safely go ahead. That meant that another car was ahead of him, going in the same direction. When he left the siding, the light on his right would always be lit, whether by him or by the preceding motorman.

This simple system, bolstered by the company's posted signs threatening prosecution for murder of anyone who tampered with the

One of the West Penn's heavier interurban cars.

switches, was most effective. The company had an excellent safety
record in all its more than half a century.

Track gauge and signaling were not the only unorthodox features of
the West Penn. Where every other line had cars with air brakes, the
West Penn main line cars used a combination of a Westinghouse
electromagnetic track brake and a gooseneck hand brake, called
"dynamic braking." If you looked under a West Penn car, you'd see
four bars of iron hanging loosely on springs between the wheels,
immediately over the rails. When a motorman wanted to stop, he
pushed his controller handle into a position that converted the motors
into electric generators, and fed the resulting current into the brakes.
The iron bars then gripped the rails, and as they went down, caused
strategically placed levers to tighten brakes on each wheel. Thus, the
faster the car was traveling, the more electric braking power it
generated. As soon as it stopped, however, the bars stopped gripping
the rails and the wheel levers lost their effectiveness. For this reason,
motormen had to use the hand brake to hold the car when it was
stopped.

The West Penn's largest system was called the "Coke Region," because it ran through the coal mine and coke area. (Coke is a fuel made by heating coal in a closed oven until the gases have been removed. It burns slowly and without smoke, and is excellent for heating and for metallurgic ovens.) The trolley line was patronized by miners going to and from the pits. Even in good times, when these workers had their own cars, they rode the trolley rather than cover the interior of what was a prized possession with the coal dust they had accumulated in a shift's work.

True to its offbeat nature, the West Penn was one of the few interurbans to overlap the age of television. To the dismay of the management, television came to the Pittsburgh area and suddenly nobody rode the trolley any more in the evening.

If it hadn't been for the peculiarity of the West Penn's gauge, it might have survived longer than it did. In that heavily industrial area, the road should have been able to develop an interchange freight relationship with the railroads. That would have given them the revenue to keep the West Penn Railways operating later than 1941, when it gave up its freight operations. This, in turn, would have allowed the passenger service to continue running. The only move in that direction was an arrangement with a truck line called Alko that served south-central Pennsylvania. But this involved moving all the freight from trolley car to truck, and that was costly.

The peculiar, long-lived, dependable, endearing West Penn! When the last car ran out of Connellsville bound for Uniontown on August 9, 1952, there was hardly a dry eye among the crowd of over 5,000 who came to bid it farewell!

7
Too Good to Last

There can be no doubt that the development of the automobile (and its fat brothers, the truck and the bus) and constant improvement of tax-supported roads killed the interurbans. *How* this happened, however, is disputed hotly. Diagnoses differ.

Everyone I have asked about it points an unwavering finger at sinister maneuvering on the part of the automobile industry—most particularly General Motors—and allied road interests. Of course, everyone I have asked happens to be heavily biased on the side of trolleys.

General Motors Executive Vice-President Oscar A. Lundin has answered to charges of trolleycide with the following defense: "The trolleys were abandoned not because of General Motors, but because of economics and inefficiency. It's common knowledge in the transit industry that their decline began more than fifty years ago."

It is true that the industry was especially vulnerable because never in its brief life was it a highly profitable or financially sound venture. Although individual entrepreneurs, such as the Everett-Moore Syndicate, made money on their lines, even the best of trolley companies, in the best of times, paid a low return on investment. A significant number of lines were already in receivership in the halcyon period when the Lake Shore Electric was carrying 2,000 passengers a day and investors were knocking one another over to get in on the boom. Although the trolleys took business from the railroads, they took the least profitable part of it—short-run passenger traffic and short-haul, less-carload freight.

The very contradiction, however, in the healthy patronage of the trolley lines and the sickly balance sheets indicate that the trolleys themselves, as physical entities, served a purpose that was not reflected in their economics. The trouble was somewhere other than on the rails.

In the beginning, when roads were unpaved and automobiles undependable, the interurban didn't need to fear competition from motor traffic. The first interurban ran in 1893; by the time of World War I, 7 million passengers a years passed through the huge terminal in Indianapolis, and 500 cars a day arrived and departed. In the late twenties and early thirties one line after another was being abandoned. "By 1933," say Hilton and Due, "the typical interurbans had collapsed." At its peak the industry contained 16,100 miles of track; by the beginning of World War I only 2,700 miles were left.

We are only belatedly learning that interurban short-haul transportation and motor car travel could have existed side-by-side, providing a genuine alternative for travelers going distances too short for airplanes. But the automobiles never had the financial burden of securing right-of-way and maintaining track; their government did that for them. (The contention that roads are financed by the taxes on gasoline is hardly accurate, according to a study a few years ago by Dr. Lyle C. Fitch of the Institute of Public Administration. If motorists who use a typical freeway at peak hours were to pay for it with their gasoline taxes, he computed, those taxes would have to be raised at least seventy-five cents a gallon. Dr. Fitch's figures have most probably been somewhat outdistanced by inflation, and the required tax increase would be closer to a dollar in the middle 1970s.)

Indeed, it was more than straightforward financial difficulties, we are learning, more than a national preference for the automobile, and more than the economic depression that was responsible for the mortality of the interurbans. It seemed as though the Great Epizootic now was raging through the electrical/mechanical trolley industry. A recent report from the Subcommittee on Antitrust and Monopoly of the Senate Judiciary Committee, "American Ground Transport" by Bradford Snell, has turned up substantial reinforcement for those who put the blame on General Motors.

When the New York, New Haven & Hartford was powered by overhead trolley wires—and look at them all! (1907)

The study shows that GM and highway interests close to the giant corporation "bought local transit companies, scrapped the pollution-free electric trains, tore down the power transmission lines, ripped up the tracks, and placed GM motor buses on already congested . . . streets. The noisy foul-smelling buses turned earlier patrons of the high-speed rail system away from public transit, and in effect, sold millions of private automobiles."

GM's attack, what is more, was not limited to replacing the trolleys with buses. General Motors manufactures the Diesel-electric engines that drive the nation's trains. Snell, in the report, tells us what few may have noticed, even though the figures are there to see:

The New Haven Railroad, he says, "During fifty years of electrified operation . . . never failed to show an operating profit. Then, in 1956, GM persuaded [the railroad] to tear down the electric lines and scrap an entire fleet of powerful highspeed electric locomotives. By 1959, three years after Dieselization, the New Haven lost $9.2 million. In 1961 it was declared bankrupt; by 1968, when it was acquired by the Penn Central, it had accumulated a deficit of nearly $300 million. After a review of these facts, the ICC in an unprecedented move, found that General Motors had contributed to the New Haven's 'financial ruin.'

"The most disturbing aspect of GM's Dieselization program," Snell continues, "is that it eliminated a technological alternative, electric trains, which would have helped the railroads compete with highway transport. Today, when *virtually every other advanced nation has electrified its trains* [italics the author's], America and what is left of America's railroads are *still* locked in to GM Diesel locos."

The trolleys didn't go down without a fight—at least on some fronts. In 1930, Dr. Thomas Conway, president of the Cincinnati & Lake Erie, whose interurban cars ran between Cincinnati, Dayton, and Columbus, and between Cincinnati and Toledo, tried to modernize his road by inaugurating new high-speed lightweight cars, half of them fitted as coaches, half as coach-observation cars. They were geared to run at higher than eighty miles an hour, and to give their passengers a comfortable ride. They were the first cars to use aluminum successfully on a large scale.

It was one of these cars, (which the promotion-minded Conway called "Red Devils") that was featured in the great trolley-car and airplane race afterwards immortalized in a poster. The trolley car won. (The aircraft involved was the slowest biplane made; still, to be able to outdo *any* plane, however slow, that could fly fast enough to stay aloft is a respectable achievement.

Dr. Conway was responsible also for the development of the most modern city streetcar design until the Boeing Vertol cars now in production. Called the "PCC," for "Presidents' Conference Car," this streetcar survives today in almost every city where trolleys still run. It came out of a meeting, called by Dr. Conway, convening the presidents of several trolley lines in the early thirties. They hoped to modernize and economize by introducing an attractice new streetcar that could be manufactured in quantity, for several cities at once, and therefore would be economical as well as efficient.

Pennsylvania law prohibited buses from establishing routes where the territory was already being satisfactorily served by trolleys, and time after time the courts decided in favor of the trolley line when a bus company was trying to gain a route. Other states gave no such protection to the rail lines. In the early twenties, the electric interurbans of Ohio brought their problems to the state capitol in Columbus, trying to get similar cooperation from the legislators. At that time, they approached the steam roads and asked them to join in their lobbying effort. The railroads refused summarily. With the lack of vision always more obvious fifty years after the fact, they refused to recognize a threat from buses. "Short interurban-style trips have to compete with bus travel," they said, "but who would want to ride a bus from Cleveland to Denver?"

Who, indeed?

Of course, many lines sank without a struggle, and there were some that were sacrificed for the greater good of the conglomerate or its equivalent. The Northern Ohio Power & Light, originally and symbolically the Northern Ohio *Traction* & Light, was killed, one observer told me, by Commonwealth & Southern, the company that eventually owned it. "They had a lot of automobile stock," he said. "They didn't want to run a competitive operation. They charged the trolley division $1,000 a day for using the new carbarn in Akron, just to drive them into bankruptcy."

There were a few lines struggling along in the 1950s, supported mainly by their freight business, but more departed in the thirties.

Usually, they departed lingeringly, rather than suddenly. But occasionally one would simply be running one day and retired without warning the next. A devout trolley fan named Frank Schlegel told me about driving out to the Midwest in 1938 to photograph some remaining trolley lines there. He stopped to visit a friend in Ohio, the plan being that they would go down to the track and take pictures of the Lake Shore Electric as it passed them. Schlegel had checked the schedules before he left, and knew just when he could safely find a passing interurban—he thought.

"Frank, you're too late," his friend told him when he arrived and eagerly began to unpack his camera. "This is Wednesday; the Lake Shore Electric closed down last Saturday."

The two men sadly went out and photographed the barred doors of the carbarns.

When a company applied to the state for permission to abandon, they had no trouble getting it. In some cases, however, there was a legal stumbling block. Many of the original easements stipulated that the right-of-way could be used only so long as it was used for trolley cars. Since many companies had followed a natural course from traction to power, and their wires were strung along the trolley right-of-way, they were obliged for months, and even years, to send one unprofitable car a day along the track just to keep the franchise.

Weeds on the right-of-way—a sad omen that the end of a line is near. Photograph by Eugene Van Dusen, courtesy of 35 Slides, Colorado Springs, Colorado.

Since trolley car factories had either closed down or converted to a product with a more promising future, there were at the end no spare parts, and the healthier lines had to resort to cannibalization, an expedient whereby one or more old cars were sacrificed to provide spare parts for their comrades. The Lake Shore Electric by 1933, five years before abandonment, had already done away with its track crews. As a young man of twenty, even then addicted to interurbans, Max Wilcox took a walk along a section of the line one day and felt it his responsibility to report to the supervisor that some of the track was simply lying on the ground, loose from the ties. "You can pick it up with your hand," he said. "You didn't pick it up, did you?" the supervisor demanded sharply. Upon being assured that the track was still lying in place, he told young Wilcox that his main concern was not to remedy the matter (which was impossible), but to keep pranksters from picking up the rails.

Salvage of an abandoned interurban line was a profitable enterprise for a Johnny-on-the-spot with some cash. An imaginative Elyria, Ohio, businessman bought up the Cleveland, Southwestern for something like $105,000 when it abandoned in 1931. He got not only the entire mileage of valuable steel track, which scrap metal dealers were happy to pay well for, but chunks of profitable real estate, a good bit of it in good town locations, the sites of carbarns, power plants, and the like.

Trolley cars were shuffled from one line to another; if abandonment was farther than the immediate horizon an owner would often spend money in the hope that improved service would bring back lost business. A few former interurban cars are running still on urban and suburban lines. Many have found work, temporarily at least, in Europe and Latin America. Local people would often buy one or two cars for a few hundred dollars apiece and turn them into chicken houses, diners, gas stations, or summer cottages. Trolley equipment was solidly built (when the lines abandoned, some trestles had to be dynamited to get them apart). Some of the cars survive today. More than the cars live on.

8
Intensive Care

A handsome booklet published by the Seashore Trolley Museum at Kennebunkport, Maine, calls the trolley "once the world's most important—and certainly the most interesting—transport vehicle." "Hear! Hear!" come the cries from around the country, making up in volume what they may lack in multiplicity. Trapped in a magic web of trolley wire, held in the enchantment of wheel on rail, there are those whose mission it is to keep the interurbans and the streetcars alive.

Devotion takes many forms. Those enthusiasts who have made themselves historians of the electric railways celebrate their rites not only by gathering and recording information, and meeting to exchange it. They inject themselves actively into history by traveling about in a dogged search for trolleys to ride and to photograph.

It was to socialize this kind of activity that Commander E.J. Quinby and his colleagues in 1934 founded the Electric Railroaders' Association. This group embraces *all* electric rail transport: trolleys, subways and "els," high-speed commuter service, electrified main line railroads. There is, though, a "caucus" within that larger group whose interest is primarily interurban trolleys, and among the members of that are Commander Quinby himself and the two-time president of the ERA and current New York office administrator, Herman Rinke.

Devotion manifests itself differently at the nearly twenty working trolley museums in the United States, where cars are not only displayed but sought out for restoration, then lovingly, and largely by

An all-brass model of the Chicago, North Shore and Milwaukee "Skokie" coach. It comes fully assembled, but not painted. The prototype used several different color schemes; the modeler can take his pick. Reproduced from the catalogue of E. Suydam & Co., Duarte, California, with their kind permission.

hand, restored, and finally operated for the satisfaction of the museum members, all volunteers, and the delight of their visitors.

Of the estimated almost 200,000 serious rail vehicle scale modelers in the country, about 12 percent of these, or 25,000, are trolley modelers. They build, to accurate scale, miniature trolley cars. They build them either from various degrees of "scratch" without any components manufactured for the purpose, with premade motors and wheel assemblies, or with purchased parts like window frames and trolley poles. They assemble them from kits, or they buy complete models and paint them. Trolley models, some of which are available in plastic and some, very occasionally, in other materials, are predominantly brass, come from Japan, and cost in the neighborhood of forty-five to seventy dollars, unpainted.

"It's a lot of money," a man named Warren Portman told me, "and that's why so many trolley modelers make their models from scratch or by kit bashing." ("Kit bashing" is a vivid expression that describes the process of taking parts from one or more model kits and creating your own car from these components.) "On the other hand," Portman went on, "there are those professional people, for instance, who have the bucks and haven't got the time. They'll come in, buy a model for sixty or seventy dollars—they won't even paint it themselves. They'll pay someone like Bob's Custom Finishers forty or fifty dollars more to paint it for them." There are even custom model builders who, for a considerable fee, will build a model for you, to your specifications.

Portman is a forthright, youngish man who began his breadwinning career as a mechanical engineer. At some point he was sidetracked into selling real estate. Meanwhile, however, he had become a model railroader, and he found his hobby taking more and more time, attention—and money. "I'm like the addict who becomes a pusher to support his habit," Portman said. "I went into the business because I couldn't afford it as a hobby any more."

Going into the business involved, at first, finding, buying, and subsequently selling, models of value that the owner wanted to part with. A great deal of trading goes on within the model railroad fraternity. And while Junior's old Lionel set might not be worth a fortune on the market, there are collectors of almost everything, and a model train from someone's attic could possibly bring a good price from Portman, or a dealer like him.

Although he now owns three model railroad stores in the New York area (called Roundhouse I, II, and III), Portman continues to trade on an individual basis. He does a lot of traveling in this activity while managers run the stores, and small dealers away from the urban centers who have access to a collection or a few cars will hold them for Portman's next visit; potential buyers contact him frequently to see what he has come up with.

These potential buyers could be straight collectors or hobbyists who run and/or build an active collection of models. Right now, in one of his two suburban shops, Portman has a collection that was created, frequently from scratch, over a period of forty years by an employee of the former New York City Transit Authority named Bernard Caldwell. Behind glass doors on the shop's shelves are railroad locomotives and passenger and freight cars, trolley cars, interurbans, horsecars, buses. Unusual items, such as an electric rail post office and a Brooklyn funeral car with deep blue curtains at the windows, alternate with typical cars from the New York City subways. There is a monorail car, called "The Monoroad," that ran a short route on the fringes of the city in 1910. There must be nearly two hundred altogether, each beautifully detailed and painted, and the traction section represents every kind of public transportation that has been seen on New York City streets since the horsecar days.

Mr. Caldwell sold his collection to Portman recently, but only after he had ascertained that it would be properly displayed, and that the

An early item on the Tappan Zee Model Railroad Club's roster: Frank W. Schlegel's meticulously made HO Indiana Service two-car train. Courtesy of Blair Foulds.

traction section would not be broken up, but sold in its entirety. His affection for the miniatures is understandable; they have a bright unusual charm that made me think, somehow, of the paintings of the Pennsylvania artist John Kane.

I talked to Portman on a Sunday afternoon in his Croton-on-Hudson, New York, store, which occupies the former Croton North Station, now abandoned by the New York Central. In his three shops (one in New York City, another in White Plains, and the original store in Croton-on-Hudson), Portman carries only the appurtenances of model railroading. "No beads, no feathers, no airplane kits, no supplies for making stained glass," he said. His approach to his business is unorthodox, but it seems to be working. This may be due, partly at least, to his own genuine interest in and knowledge of model railroading, and to his very apparent friendliness and effort to oblige. "I don't want to get mean," he says. "Some of the people I've run into in this business are really mean."

Unusual is his discount policy, which he follows in order to compete with the large discount chains. It is the only way, he feels, to build up the volume that makes the business pay. He suits his hours to those of his customers, staying open a half hour later than most other shops on his street in the city, and maintaining evening and Sunday hours in the suburban stores.

As we talked, people came and went in the shop. They priced brass models of trolley cars, bought HO scale wall clocks (thirty cents), wall phones (twenty-five cents), or cuspidors (fifteen cents) for their layouts, thumbed through old copies of *Railroad* magazine, examined some of the hundreds of kits on the shelves. The phone rang several times: Are you open? How late will you stay open? Do you buy models? A young couple came in with some toy trains wrapped in a cloth. Portman examined them and said matter-of-factly that they weren't of any value; the couple obviously had acquired them somewhere without knowing anything about them.

Through the window, we could see part of the extensive New York Central tracks at Croton North. It was in this complex that the trains used to change from steam to electric engines, so as not to have the steam, or later, the Diesel exhaust in the tunnel that runs under Manhattan to Grand Central Station.

Suddenly, there was an unmistakable hoot of a locomotive horn, and a loco went slowly by, the engineer waving broadly from his cab window. Portman waved just as broadly back.

"That's Big Joe," he said. "He runs the big trains during the day and the little ones at night. You'd be surprised how many railroad men are model railroaders."

Although Portman opened his New York City store across the street from one of the largest "railroad only" hobby shops in the United States, he has been clever enough to complement their stock rather than compete with it. He doesn't sell, for example, such items as decalcomanias, which require an enormous inventory. Decals are necessary to every modeler, whether he scratch builds, uses kits, or buys his models and paints them; very few people have the talent to letter well enough to approximate the legends on the sides of cars, or copy in small scale the insignia of the different roads. "When someone comes in and asks for decals," Portman says, "I tell him to go to our parts department across the street!" On the other hand, he carries many items that his competitors do not.

Portman's success with his model shops bears out a survey done by *Model Railroader* magazine recently that revealed that about $45 million a year was spent on goods for that hobby.

An allied business—one that has a branch devoted to trolleys and that seems to be staffed almost entirely with entrepreneurs who are railfans first and business people after that—is specialty publishing in the field. Books, magazines, and such incidentals as postcards, posters, and calendars, roll off the presses around the country. The Central Electric Railfans Association in Chicago publishes books about Midwest trolleys in the ten-to-twenty-five-dollar range—books with titles like *Electric Railways of Northeastern Ohio, Badger Traction: The Story of the Smaller Electric Railways of Wisconsin*, ets.—and finds a hefty market for such electric-railroadiana. (Since Hilton and Due list over 700 interurban lines, a large percentage of them in the Midwest, the CERA has a long way to go before it runs out of railways to publish books about.)

The Connecticut Valley chapter of the National Railway Historical Society, although partial to steam and Diesel railroads, does devote fairly frequent issues of its one dollar publication, *Transportation*, to company histories of interurban lines.

With the same avidity with which a baseball fan collects batting averages, earned run averages, and arcane records ("the first left-handed-hitting, right-throwing pitcher to commit two balks in one season in a city beginning with 'C' ") trolley fans delight in documentation. A favorite topic is a detailed history, with photographs, of some departed trolley company. Often a ferocious attachment to an obscure, forgotten (and never very conspicuous) interurban line will move an amateur historian to produce a book. While physically in the small-potatoes category, with hand-typed composition and rather murky photos, these histories are always thoroughly researched, frequently competently organized, and well written.

At the other extreme is the large number of fairly to very well designed and printed high-priced books from publishers like Kalmbach and Carstens. Newton Gregg, a West Coast firm, specializes in handsome reprints of unusual specialized books, among them *The Electric Railway Dictionary* and a series called *Train Shed Cyclopedia*.

Kalmbach and Carstens, and smaller publishers as well, put out shelves of how-to's: *Easy-to-Build Model Railroad Structures, HO Primer*, track plans, and blueprints.

Writing and publishing articles and books on traction is an act of devotion. The occupation seems almost invariably to come *after* a long-time love affair with the trolleys rather than as a result of a writer's having cast about for a likely subject. Certainly the publishers or authors on trolley subjects are as well known for being enthusiasts as they are as word-polishers. Professor Alan L. Rice, who specializes in writing about traction subjects in the Philadelphia area; Joe Diaz, who publishes *Street Railway Journal*; Vane Jones, whose magazine is called *Traction and Models*, all are experts in the field. Vane's company also reprints *Traction Heritage*, a bimonthly of excerpts from the *Electric Railway Journal* of the first years of this century, and these are only some of his trolley-related activities. Richard Wagner makes O-scale components of great exactitude, and with his wife Birdella publishes *Trolley Talk*. William Middleton's hardcover books on trolleys are on library shelves everywhere. The names of Roger Borrup, James D. Johnson, Harold Cox, W. R. Gordon, Vincent Seyfried, Randolph Kulp, Joseph Canfield, O. R. Cummings may be absent from the best-seller lists, but to trolley fans, they are as well known (or better!) than Jacqueline Susann and James Michener.

Jim Businger, the "hardware" collector, enjoys his "pieces" of trolley cars for the history they evoke. I met another collector, who seemed to approach his hobby from a different direction. Arnold Berman enjoys *having* his model trolleys, he enjoys working toward owning a complete roster of every model trolley car made, and is never happier than when acquiring a new model or piece of trolley "paper," as collectors call photographs, timetables, advertisements, dispatching instructions, and the like.

I went to see Berman at the suggestion of Warren Portman, who told me that Bernard Caldwell, the creator of the delightful model collection at the Roundhouse, had sold Berman an immense library of photographs documenting the New York City transit system, and that while these were out of my immediate area, Berman also had a great deal of trolley material I should see.

I phoned Berman and he gave me directions to his house. "It's near the Heathcote stop of the New York, Westchester & Boston," he said.

(The NY,W&B is an electric railroad that died in 1937 and that never made it any closer to Boston than White Plains and Portchester, both about twenty miles from the starting point.) "I'll be glad to show you what I have," said Berman, "but it's all over the place."

He couldn't have described it more accurately. As a sideline to his profession as controller for a large hotel, Berman sells trolley models by mail, in collaboration with a Connecticut manufacturer/importer named Bert Sas, whose firm is Fairfield Models. Berman does this from a small room in his paneled and carpeted basement. It has a desk, and a shelf for an HO layout is built around two walls. A third wall is completely covered with stacks of transfile boxes. Another has shelves and bookshelves. Every surface in the room (including most of the floor) is piled high with objects. Papers, boxes containing models, magazines, books, models sitting out on the desk and the track layout—the eyes bug, the mind reels.

I picked my way over to the chair Berman indicated, and he told me something about his activities. He has almost stopped collecting trolleys, he said, because he now has everything being currently made; it is just a matter of being sure he gets anything new that comes out. He is interested in locomotives, now, and has some rare models. Among them is a Santa Fe locomotive made by an artisan now dead, the value of which, he told me, is in the neighborhood of $800. He explained that the lettering and insignia on this man's locos were done freehand, not with decals, and that there is no one else who has the ability to do this—the art is lost. (I thought of all the recent art school graduates with drafting talent, who can letter beautifully, and could copy anything, and resolved to advise them to look into model railroading.)

Berman has never made a model himself; he is a collector and dealer only. He does run his trolleys occasionally on someone else's layout, and plans to do this on his own HO track as soon as he gets it cleared off—a project he has been working on for several years.

What he possesses is a genuine love and appreciation of the well-made models that he owns and sells; dozens and dozens of them fill the shelves in his office and in an adjacent closet, each one carefully packed in sponge-rubber-lined cartons. His standards are extremely high, and he combines an acute eye for quality with a talent for finding a good buy, if not a bargain. His collection includes not only the hand-

9
Trolley Jollies and Juice Jacks

The premises of the Electric Railroaders Association at 145 Greenwich Street, just north of New York's Wall Street area, have their own character. Models of trolleys and high-speed electric rail cars sit on ledges and desk tops and windowsills. Photographs of subway and trolley cars enliven the walls. The place has the fusty air of an office that is maintained by the principals of an organization, without support staffs of secretaries and clerical flunkeys to camouflage its purpose with a layer of commercial elegance. It is a roll-top desk environment; one of multi-drawered olive green metal filing cabinets and piles of magazines.

Presiding over the office is Herman Rinke, who has twice been elected the organization's president, and now is an official of the New York chapter.

Mr. Rinke became a railroader when he was taken on as an office boy at the headquarters of the New York Central Railroad. He left the position to which he had risen in the accounting office to go, first to college and then to Yale for a graduate degree in transportation.

The next two years saw him in Idaho, working for the Great Northern Railroad. Although a steam road, the Great Northern ran its trains through the Cascade Mountains on electric power until they were Dieselized in 1941. It is accurate, then, to say that Rinke is an electric railroad man.

The Electric Railroaders Association's interests embrace everything in electric railroading: street trolleys, interurbans, mass

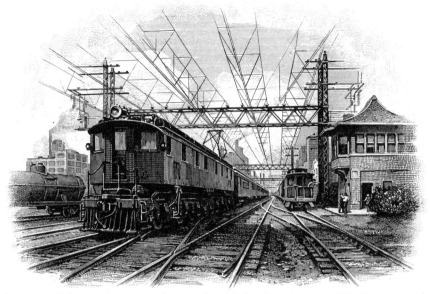

Favorite of the juice jacks—a heavy electrified railroad train, 1931. Courtesy of American Bank Note Company.

transit—subways and "els" and rapid suburban trains—and electrified railroads. This last is the category of railroads that have replaced their steam or Diesel engines with heavy electric locomotives. (The particular enthusiasts who concentrate on these are called "juice jacks.") Without prejudice, but a bit mischievously, Rinke explained that, in theory, even Diesel-electric locomotives are really electric engines that carry their own power plant with them; the Diesel simply generates the power that runs the train, rather than an outside plant's doing it. That is true, of course, and yet—and yet—. The ERA eschews Diesel electrics, as they do the trolley buses, which, although powered by electricity, do not run on rails.

Since Commander E. J. Quinby and his friends founded the ERA in 1934, it has had 4,960 members, Rinke tells me. At present, there are about 2,200 dues-paying members; most of them are in the United States, most of them on the East Coast, but a few chime in now and then from abroad. The association sends its newsletter to every continent in the world but one. "We used to have a member in Africa," Rinke told me. "But we haven't heard from him in a long time."

Herman Rinke found electric railroads in the west, too. Here is one, western style (1932). Courtesy of American Bank Note Company.

The ERA has appropriate books for sale—lists of them. It also has jigsaw puzzle maps of the New York City subway system, the Paris Metro, the London Underground, and the Montreal subway. Mr. Rinke showed me *Headlights*, a neat bulletin of a dozen pages with signed stories detailing current events in electric transportation and lots of well reproduced black-and-white photographs. "That's the crack in the wall," he said. "*Headlights*. People join us so they can get *Headlights*, then they start coming around, going on fan trips, taking pictures—and we've got them!

"I see a pattern for our members." He thumbed through the card files in the flat drawers of a metal cabinet. "They come to us as young people—in high school or a little after. They're active for a while, and then they get busy with college, get jobs, get married, have children—they haven't time for us. But when all that is over, they come back."

A member is never dropped from the ERA. Unless he resigns in writing, he is considered a member, albeit, if he drops from sight and pays no dues, a "dormant" one. Any time he pays back dues, he is reinstated, and *Headlights* again appears in his mailbox each month.

Rinke spends much of his non-job time at the ERA, and has been with it almost from the very beginning. He stayed two years with the Great Northern, traveling in the Rockies and the Cascades. He told me about stopping overnight where the guests in the small town's only hotel were given oil lanterns as they retired. Since the hotel seemed quite adequately lit by electricity, he asked why the lantern. The manager explained that Jake, who owned the garage, was also the proprietor of the town generator.

"When he goes to bed," she said, "he turns it off for the night. We don't want anybody to break his neck on the way to the bathroom!"

"The wide open spaces are fine," Herman Rinke said, reminiscing about his western days. "But after a while you can get pretty tired of them. I was born and raised in New York, and I wanted to come back."

It is understandable, then, why Herman Rinke regarded with amusement and wonder the two women tourists he encountered on one of the Great Northern trains. The train was rolling through the Cascade Mountains, one of the more spectacular areas on the North American Continent. Sheer ancient walls rose around them, and through gaps in these nearby mountains, other earth and rock giants filled the view.

The two women sat staring in front of them, stern-faced and disapproving.

"First time out here?" asked Rinke of the two. One gave no sign of having heard; the other favored Rinke with a slight and miserly nod. But he persisted. "Where are you from?" he asked. "Kansas," mumbled the talkative one.

"Are you enjoying the trip?"

That did it. "No, we are not!" she said emphatically. When pressed, she told him why. "In Kansas, we can look out and see our neighbors six miles away. Here there's nothing to see!"

The Electric Railroad Association members are not model makers—or at least, not in their role as Electric Railroaders. Some of them do build models, of course, and some have an interest in the restoration of trolley cars, but it certainly isn't a function of the organization. Instead, they meet, they talk, and they show their photographs and moving pictures of electric cars and trains they have known. Like big-game hunters, they have spent decades, some of them, stalking about the country, with camera if not gun, seeking the elusive interurban, tracking the trolley car, lying in wait for the high-speed subway train that will come snorting through the tunnel and be snapped by the cocked camera. The catch is displayed at the regular membership meetings.

They have fan trips, too. Four or five or six times a year, members gather to ride a special train, photographing as they go. Usually, nowadays, it is a subway train or some similar everyday vehicle, although to ride on a railfan trip is a bit different from hopping from Times Square to 72nd Street on the Broadway Seventh Avenue subway.

The weekend reserved for the Electric Railroaders' Association convention is that closest to July 4. Annual film programs resurrect old lines and recall trips taken long ago. At the Saturday night banquet, speeches are given by old ERA members who have moved ahead in the world of transportation—an astonishing percentage. "I don't know," said Rinke, "of any electric transportation system that doesn't have a few of our members in career positions."

One of the most notable fan experts is George Krambles, who is superintendent of operations for the Chicago Transit System. Krambles founded the Central Electric Railfans Association. His day-to-day job deals with mass transit. His heart is with the interurbans still, and his enthusiasm all-embracing. A friend tells me about the time he was driving with Krambles somewhere in the Chicago area and Krambles insisted that they stop at one of the yards under his supervision. Krambles pulled a camera from the glove box, jumped out of his car, and began snapping pictures.

The high point of a recent ERA convention was George Krambles's description of a trip to Japan to see the high-speed Takaido Express. "You take your children to see the crack train here in Chicago," Krambles told the group, "and you have a choice of just one, the Broadway Limited; you can see it once a day. Japan has an electric railroad that makes seventy runs a day!"

The applause was deafening.

Several ERA members have gone into the specialized publishing that reaches railfans: *Model Railroader, Trains, Railway Model Craftsman.* The late Ira Swett created a truly staggering series of illustrated histories of the West Coast interurbans—a series that is being continued by a former collaborator. George Horn, who began as a motorman in New York City mass transit, is now yardmaster for the system; and the heads of the big railroad publishing houses, Hal Carstens of Carstens and Al Kalmbach of Kalmbach, are both ERA members.

"I'll tell you why so many of our people are in important positions all around the country," an ERA member said recently. "We're the only people who know how to run a railroad!"

"When we were kids," Herman Rinke told me, "most people considered trolley cars just a nuisance. If you were a 'trolley jolly'—that's what everyone called them—you were a little bit embarrassed about it. But it was the trolley jollies who saved the lines when they were talking about closing them down. If we heard a rumor that some runs were going to be canceled, we'd get on a streetcar, ride for a while, get out and start passing around literature that said 'Save your trolley line!' Well, those people used the line, and once we got them stirred up, they did save a lot of runs.

"Now," he went on, "we're justified. Boston and San Francisco have each ordered about two hundred new cars. They call them Light Rail Vehicles, now—LRV's—but they're trolley cars. Boeing Vertol is supposed to be making them—I only hope they know how!"

"Why wouldn't they?" I asked.

"Just haven't got the experience," Rinke said.

He went on to talk about BART—Bay Area Rapid Transit, the system running in San Francisco, and from Oakland and Berkeley to San Francisco.

"They threw away the Key System," Rinke said. "They had a perfectly good system that went over Oakland Bay by the Oakland/San Francisco Bay Bridge. It used cab signals, because it was frequently so foggy over the bay that wayside signals would have been invisible."

Although Key System cars could do only about thirty-five miles an hour over the Bay, and the BART speeds along at seventy-five miles an hour in a tunnel *under* it, Mr. Rinke feels that with foresight the Key System rails could have been kept, and now it would be possible to reinstate the service, in modernized form that achieves high speed at moderate cost and with good safety. BART, he feels, isn't sufficiently fail safe, and the experience of the system so far has borne him out. There have been three collisions, two with passengers aboard; Rinke says they were due to bad engineering. He deplores the fact that it took five to six years longer than originally estimated to build the BART,

The Key System was the forerunner of the Oakland-Berkeley-San Francisco BART, and is in some ways a suburban service and in some ways interurban. This articulated car is now at the California Railway Museum, Rio Vista Junction, Solano County. Photograph by Addison H. Laflin, Jr. Courtesy of the Bay Area Electric Railroad Association.

and it cost twice as much as planned. Service is limited—at the time I spoke to him, the system stopped running daily at 8 P.M. and had only just then instituted weekend service. Fares are high, and a few weeks after Herman Rinke had told me all this, there was a story in the newspapers saying that about 20 percent of the BART cars were out of service and being repaired at any given time.

Rinke summed it up. "They build an El," he said scornfully, "and call it an 'aerial structure'! Aerial structures!"

Our conversation soon wandered back to more congenial subjects, and he made the point that the candy story interurban stations were, far from a drawback, part of the early success of the lines. "People constantly saw the interurban going through the streets of the town," he said. "They were reminded of it all the time, and it was convenient to get to the stops. They didn't have to go to the outskirts of town to get on the cars, the way they did with the steam lines."

(Now, of course, they have to go to the very farthest outskirts of town to get the planes that are the principal means of transportation between cities.)

"The trolley passes through towns and villages," said an early ad for an interurban line in the Chicago area. "The steam road skirts them."

The hour was getting late; I was going to have to come back another time to see the Sprague Library. Founded by the ERA, named for the man who made the electric trolley possible, it is perhaps the most extensive collection in the world of books, magazines, maps, photographs, statistics, and other historical and current documents dealing with electric railways. "History, service and progress" is the ERA's motto, and the maintenance and expansion of the library is one way they carry this out.

Commander Quinby says he and other kindred spirits formed the Electric Railroaders Association because they loved the electric railway and "viewed its past with affection and its future with courage and ambition."

Certainly, the same attitude applies to all that Herman Rinke has to say about electric railroading in general, and interurban railroading in particular. It is with affection that he shares with you his broad knowledge of the whole colorful interurban time, and it is with courage and ambition that he embraces the possibility of the return of the trolleys.

10
Riding to Scale

Model railroading is, of course, a highly popular hobby; everyone knows at least one person who has "electric trains," which means models of steam or Diesel locomotives and the cars they pull. Actually, of course, these miniature steam and Diesel locos are powered by electricity in the rails themselves.

Those who model, run, or play with small electric trolleys are a rarer breed. Have you ever heard of a child's getting a set of "electric *streetcars*" for Christmas—much less toy interurbans! (It is interesting to note, however, that the Lionel Company was making toy or "tinplate" electric streetcars as early as 1904, and the Carlisle and Finch Company of Cincinnati pictured both streetcars and interurban trolleys in their 1900 catalogue.) The trolley modeler marches to a different drummer. He shares a fierce devotion—and his technical problems—with the dedicated few.

The absolute *sine qua non* of modeling is that it be accurately to scale. Modelers have a choice of O scale, which is slightly more than 1/4 inch to the foot, HO (Half-O) which is, consequently, a hairline over 1/8 inch to the foot. (An even smaller scale, N, about half the size of HO or 1/16 inch to the foot, is gaining popularity among railroad modelers, but I don't know of any trolley models being made in N.) Of course, there is no reason a model maker can't choose any scale he likes, but the more esoteric he becomes, the slimmer his chance of being able to find any manufactured material to help him in his work.

No. 1-R. Electric Railway, with Reversible Motor.

PRICE, $4.00.

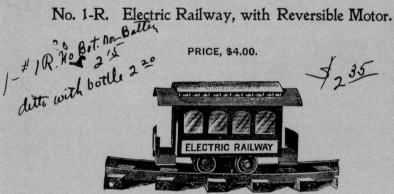

As it is often desired to run our No. 1 Motor Car in either direction, we have brought out our NO. 1-R RAILWAY. This railway is the same as our No. 1 in every respect, except the Motor. This latter has a three-pole armature, and a reversing switch is provided for reversing the motor, stopping and starting, etc.

Size of car, length of track, gauge of track, battery, etc., same as the No. 1 Railway.

Weight, packed in wooden box, 6 pounds.

MOTOR CAR only, $3.25.

F. M. CAMPBELL,
Dealer in
General Merchandise and Farm Implements.

Lexington, Ind., Aug. 7, 1899.
The Carlisle & Finch Co., Cincinnati.
Gentlemen :
It is a fine little machine for the money.
Yours truly,
ARTIE CAMPBELL,
Box 2.

257 E. Eighty-Sixth St., New York City, N. Y.,
October 7, 1900.
The Carlisle & Finch Co., Cincinnati, O.
Dear Sirs:.
I must say that the dynamos you make are as perfectly made as a watch. I bought one of your $7.50 dynamos which run by water power, of a dealer in New York City, and I am well satisfied.
Yours,
HARRY C. TIETJEN.

There was a time—1900 in this case—when kids were given "electric trolleys" instead of "electric trains." Even then, the grownups were apt to take over. The above Carlisle & Finch catalogue from that year reproduces some of the adult testimonials.

W. 1 - #2 motor + truck 1 30

No. 2. Electric Railway, with Double Truck Car.

#2 no battery 3 60
1 - #2 with bottle but no battery 3 70
1 - #2

PRICE, $6.50.

4 00

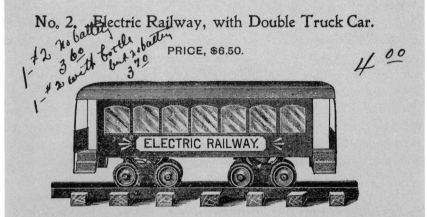

ELECTRIC RAILWAY.

This railway is made to meet the demands for a larger and more elaborate equipment than our small four-wheel car. It has 18 feet of steel track, 2-inch gauge, which may be arranged in any shape to suit purchaser. The car is 12 inches long, 5 inches high, and 3½ inches wide. It is made of metal and has iron wheels. Two motors (one on each truck) enable it to haul trail cars and climb considerable grades. Speed of car about 150 feet per minute.

The entire equipment consists of car, 18 feet of track, five zinc-carbon elements, and two ten-ounce bottles of Chromite. Use ordinary tumblers for battery cells. We do not furnish these, on account of extra weight and danger of breakage in shipment.

Where it is desired to run this car on electric light current, refer to page 13 for diagram of connections, etc.

Weight, complete, in box, 10 pounds.

3.25

MOTOR CAR only, $5.00.

.90 TRAIL CAR, same size and style as Motor Car No. 2, $1.50. If sent by mail the postage will be 44 cents additional.

Zincs (set of five), 20 cents. By mail 25 cents.

Ten-ounce bottle of Chromite, 20 cents. Can not be sent by mail.

.25 Twenty-ounce bottle of Chromite, 35 cents. Can not be sent by mail.

.80 Five-pound jar of Chromite, $1.00. Can not be sent by mail.

.18 Track and ties in 9-ft. lengths, 35 cents. By mail, 50 cents.

1 - 5 cell Battery 35 ¢

The railroad modeler lays rails and connects them to the power supply. His trains run on an electric current across both rails of his track.

The trolley modeler must plan and plant power poles over his track to carry the wire. The poles, depending on the terrain of his layout, are about 3.7" high in HO scale, 7.4" in O. He (rarely is it "she") must string wires over the track, using very small hardware—the "frogs" that divert a trolley from one wire to another at a switch are 5/16" x 5/64" for both gauges, not strictly in scale—but more about that later.

He must then control the delicate arrangements that allow his tiny trolley pole to apply just enough pressure on the wire to pick up the current without pushing it out of place. The smaller the model, the more critical this balance is.

One of the first serious trolley modelers—and one still very much involved with the craft—is Blair Foulds, who models in HO scale. I first met Mr. Foulds at the Branford Trolley Museum in Connecticut, where I was introduced to him by Frank Schlegel, the museum's official photographer and an expert veteran model maker himself, whose beautiful small trolleys have won a stack of prizes over almost forty years. Schlegel told me that Blair Foulds had the layout that I should see if I wanted to write about interurbans, and I later found that whenever I mentioned my interest to anyone in the area remotely connected with the hobby, I was told, "There's a man named Blair Foulds. . . ." One hobby shop owner cried, "He *is* traction modeling! He's the *father* of traction modeling!"

He is also a wonderfully friendly, intelligent, and knowledgeable man who has been as helpful and informative as anyone could be about this field in which he is so thoroughly versed. A tall and articulate retired engineer, a widower, Foulds lives alone in a shipshape house in New York's Westchester County. When I paid my first visit to him, he took me out to the screened porch in the rear to show me some tuberous begonias with which he was struggling and which were behaving mysteriously. Gardening, however, is a minor activity; Foulds keeps extremely occupied in a broad area of trolley and trolley modeling.

It is to Foulds's advantage in his hobby that he has had a lengthy background in engineering work of all kinds. He introduced to the public the first home tape recorder, and has played a role in a number of other ingenious scientific/engineering developments.

This General Electric interurban freight locomotive built by Blair Foulds in 1935 is believed to be the first of the HO trolleys ever made that operated from an overhead wire. Built entirely of brass, from scratch, it originally contained a homemade drive mechanism, which was later replaced by a commercial one. It is still running on Fould's layout, and was appropriately honored on its fortieth anniversary. Photograph by Frank W. Schlegel. Collection of Blair Foulds.

On his living room coffee table that first evening was a partly finished model of one of the interurban cars that ran in Pennsylvania's Lehigh Valley during the early 1900s. Foulds commented that it was an unusual project of him, since it was in the larger O scale. He was building the model, from kit parts that he was adapting because the kit was not quite to his liking, in order to have something to take with him when he visited friends with O layouts. "When I go to see Ernie Snow, in New Haven," he said, "it would be nice to have something to run with his trains." Snow has literally hundreds of O scale models he has made from scratch, and is known as one of the most prolific of model makers in the country as well as one of the most skilled.

Foulds built his first model electric trolley vehicle in 1935, an HO steeplecab locomotive of brass that is still robustly rolling about on his track layout. It is believed to be the first HO trolley-operated model ever built. (The model trolley cars made in finished form before that—and there were a very few—were sham trolleys only; they ran off electricity in the rails like the electric trains—what the trolley

This model car was scratch-built; the trestle it stands on was scratch-built. Both were made by Blair Foulds. Both are rolling stock of the Tappan Zee Model Railroad Club. Collection of Blair Foulds.

builders call a "two-rail operation.") In the spring of 1975 his hobbyist friends held a proper celebration to mark the fortieth anniversary of Blair Foulds's steeplecab loco.

"There are two ways to make model trolleys," Foulds told me. "You can make them after prototypes—in other words, make an exact scale replica of some particular car that actually existed and ran. Or you can create your own trolley line; where you build cars that are authentic models of a particular type of actual trolley car, but then paint them with your own livery and letter them with the name of your own line."

As it turned out, the latter is what his O model finally was—a car on Foulds's own "Central States Electric Line." Because he felt the kit was not faithful to its stated prototype, he had adapted it from the original kit to such a degree that he took over the finished car for his own line.

Foulds has, among his more than two hundred trolley models, some HO models that are made from scratch (except for the motors and possibly the wheel trucks), some from kits, and all sorts of types in between where he has adapted kit elements to his own design. He has bought still other models, most of them of brass, complete, except for painting, from one or another manufacturer.

Many of his models, as well as those of other hobbyists, are the result of "kit bashing"—building a car from a serendipity of sources: parts of two or more kits, pieces of kits changed by the model builder, pieces used in places other than where they were intended, and handmade components or bits of discarded cars.

The layout in Foulds's basement is, he says, very simple, although to the untutored eye it is wildly complicated. On waist-high shelves against walls painted with the silhouette of trees and blue sky, the tracks form, basically, a double set of *U*s going from the end of one leg of the *U* to the end of the other, with a loop at either end to allow the cars to get back to where they started without having to be removed from the track and turned around by a hand from above. Over all stretches the trolley wire; sometimes a single wire, sometimes a catenary, a wire suspended from another above it or to the side of it.

There are numerous stops, which give this simple plan its air of complexity. There are two major "yards"—concatenations of tracks side by side, and absolutely imperative as storage space for the enormous number of trolley cars of various sorts in Foulds's collection.

Among them I spotted several I recognized as miniatures of interurbans that had seen actual service. The lovely arched-window cars of the Illinois Terminal Railroad were there in force, and Foulds confided that the Illinois Terminal is his favorite line.

Frank Schlegel, who had joined us, said, "I've got good news for you, Blair. I heard that there are going to be four Illinois Terminal cars available from Suydam pretty soon." Suydam, he explained, is a West Coast supplier who deals exclusively in trolley models and their appurtenances.

"Wouldn't I like to get my hands on those," Foulds said. "They'll cost a fortune, though."

The cars in question would include one of those special cars the Illinois Terminal was almost unique in having, a trolley sleeping car. The promised models would be of brass, made in Japan, highly detailed, and would cost probably about sixty-five or seventy dollars apiece, judging from what I had seen of similar models. Foulds would paint them himself, either (and probably) with the Illinois Terminal livery or with that of his own Central States Electric Line.

The CSEL, Blair Foulds believes, is "the oldest line in model traction that is more or less continuously operating." The livery is trolley orange, with a green roof and red doors; the finished models are a fleet of trim little cars that do their owner proud.

Foulds has not only named his line; he has given distinctive names to the communities along his track. Spotted along the 450 feet of layout are stations that are the centers of small villages. Each station is named for one of Foulds's model traction friends: "Warren," "Ledgard," "Roy," "Finnerty," "Gilcher," "Schlegel," "Snow"; each has a neatly lettered sign so indicating. Although Foulds does not make his own structures on the layout, as many model makers do, he has found a wide variety of snap-together kits. Churches, stores of all descriptions, houses, garages, barns—he has compiled accurate representations of the small towns on an old-time interurban route. With the same single decalcomania letters he uses on many of his cars, he has doctored the signs on these buildings, the advertising signs on the sides of a barn, or the shingles over a store, to incorporate fond

Blair Foulds has an oil refinery on his layout because he likes to run tank cars. Collection of Blair Foulds.

jokes at his friends' expense. There is, for instance, "Schlegelschlofpz Beer" and the "Somers National Bank"—the latter created for his long-time modeler friend Richard Somers of New Haven. The bank, the sign over the door boasts, has assets of $100,000,000,000, and the assets were limited only, Foulds told me, by the width of the door!

One of the stops is an oil refinery, convincing with its tanks and stacks. "I've got that," confessed Foulds, "because I like oil tank cars."

At one end of the layout, reached by a feeder line, there is a small village laid out, with several streets. Foulds had added that to his over-the-country layout in order to give himself a setting for the comparatively few street trolleys he has built.

He ran some of the cars for me, explaining that their motion was a bit ragged at first because he hadn't had them running for a couple of days; in that time, enough dirt and dust will collect on the power wire to obstruct the trolley's contact.

The whole problem of electrical contact is a very good illustration of the active nature of this hobby and the complexities that can be involved. The small size of the models multiplies difficulties, but it is the care with which every detail is reproduced that makes the hobby so absorbing.

In HO scale, it takes 1/4 ounce of pressure to make contact, and at the same time, 1/4 ounce is the exact maximum you can put on the wire. A tiny spring at the base of the trolley pole regulates the exact pressure. (The prototypes use a spring, or, sometimes, a pneumatic arrangement.)

HO modelers have always had problems making the proper contact. Recently, however, a solution suggested itself rather by accident. HO gauge modelers used to substitute a flat "shoe" for the trolley wheel at the top of the pole, covering it with a sham wheel for an authentic appearance. The shoe slid along the wire, and theoretically should have given a better, firmer contact. (In actual trolley operation it does.)

Blair Foulds, working on another project with a model that had an operative trolley wheel, found that he got a much better and more consistent electrical contact. He reasoned, after investigating further, that the shoe pushed dust and minute corrosion along the wire, causing miniature arcing so tiny as not to be noticeable to the eye. The resultant sparks left very minute "cinders" on the wire, which eventually built up into a more serious interference with the contact.

Anxious to share his discovery, Foulds wrote this experience up for the National Model Railroad Association bulletin, which has let to an effort to develop new standards. Oh yes, indeed there are standards for trolley modeling.

Foulds got involved with standards early on. The Tappan Zee Model Railroad Club, of which he and Frank Schlegel, among others, were charter members, was probably one of the very earliest HO modeling clubs in the country, and quite certainly the first with a lengthy trolley line in addition to its two-rail trackage. Learning of the club, the editor of *Model Railroader* magazine wrote to Foulds asking him what the club's trolley standards were.

Foulds responded by sending drawings of a trolley "frog" he had developed—a minute bit of hardware that shunts the trolley from one line to another while the wheels are busy switching tracks down below. In a distant precursor of his present activity, he also included a drawing of the club's shoe standards. Both were dated October, 1940, and appeared in the August 1941, issue of the magazine. Both sets of standards later became incorporated into the first National Model Railroad trolley standards a few years later, and are *still* there.

Foulds has friends all over over the country who have been modeling nearly as long as he, and many of these prefer to work in O scale. He anticipated, therefore, being called upon to use his new O scale car quite often; this charming man is, as might be expected, much in demand as a guest.

Ernest Snow, one of his New Haven, Connecticut, modeler companions, has achieved the entire roster of the Sacramento Northern Railway, a large line in California that used a great variety of different types of equipment. Old wooden Niles cars, observation car/diners, freight cars and motors, heavy late interurbans—Snow has built them all, from scratch. His awards from the annual Model Railroad convention are an equally annual institution, and he once built a model interurban car, from the ground up, during one day as a convention demonstration.

In New Haven, Foulds could stop in on another friend, Bob Hoffman, who also wins prizes for his O scale models.

Should he find himself in Philadelphia, he will be able to exercise his large trolley on the tracks of John Derr, and of David Cope, both longtime trolley modelers. If he should take a trip to Boston, David Waddington will accommodate his old friend's Central States Electric car. But when he leaves for Detroit, he should remember to pack an HO model or two also, because that is where two veteran HO modelers, Harry Darst and Harry Erkfitz, both in the hobby almost as long as Foulds, run their interurban trolleys.

Occasionally, one will find a modeler who works in a larger scale—1/2 inch to the foot, or 1/24th actual size. If a trolley car prototype is 45 feet long, in 1/2" scale modeling it will be just under 2 feet. This is a large model, and for the modeler whose primary interest is in the "scratch" construction of highly detailed, very realistic cars, it is an excellent size. (He had better be prepared for modeling from the ground up, however, because I know of no 1/2" scale material that is available from manufactures.)

One such model maker—and a master model maker—is Capt. Herbert Dosey, one of the first interurban men I met when I began to learn about the subject. Captain Dosey is a large, pleasant, ruddy-faced man with white hair. In his youth, he had worked briefly as an electrical engineer on the Cleveland, Southwestern & Columbus

Model of car #36 of the Dayton and Troy line, built by Capt. Herbert Dosey. Dosey builds to ½ scale (1/24 actual size). This is large, as scale modeling goes, and Dosey makes everything on his cars, with the exception of one aluminum part, by himself. Dosey's #36 and his sixteen other cars run on the two-room layout in his Cleveland home. Photograph courtesy of Herbert Dosey.

Railway, which was one of the larger lines that ran out of Cleveland. Captain Dosey also holds merchant ship master's papers, and has been in command of the steamers that ply the Great Lakes. He has been the director of the Vermilion, Ohio, Marine Museum, to which he has contributed ship and boat models that he built. In the basement of his frame house he has an impressive collection of model interurban cars he has made himself, from blueprints he drew.

Captain Dosey chose the 1/2" scale, he says, because he could give his models greater detail and more realistic operation. He also liked the large models because they gave him room to locate the motors within the wheel trucks as they are on the prototypes, rather than having to fill the inside of the cars with them, as HO modelers must do. His models are outstanding in a field of unusual objects; except for one aluminum part made by a professional model maker, they are as scratch-built as it is possible for them to be unless Captain Dosey had gone out to fell the trees and mine the metal himself.

The captain first designs his cars to railway standards, drawing up a complete set of blueprints. He then builds them from the raw materials, even to the metal wheels and the small motors that turn the wheels. It takes Dosey seven or eight months to build a model. He uses poplar and basswood, close-grained woods that give the best finish and can be kept most closely to the desired dimensions. The truck frames are brass, the wheels cold rolled steel.

Because the motors aren't bulking in the cars' interiors, Captain Dosey can make the inside of his beautiful trolleys as realistic as the outside. He constructs small seats, and every detail of lamps, spittoons, and window shades is lovingly captured. In the motorman's vestibule you can see the controller, the air brakes, the hand brakes. The floor is covered just the way you would have seen it on an interurban trip half a century ago, and the lush interior wall paneling mimics the prototype.

Captain Dosey's cars are the green and gold striped colors of the old Cleveland, Southwestern. To achieve the gleaming finish on the outside, he puts on, successively, varnish, two coats of gray and green oil paint, the gold striping, numbering and lettering that designates his own model line, the "Lake Erie and Southern," and a final coat of varnish. The rolling stock of that line is now eleven cars; the first one, car #34, was built in 1940. Every car is a gem of realistic detail.

Captain Dosey took me down the stairs to see the Lake Erie and Southern run. His track layout covers most of two basement rooms, passing through a tunnel cut in one wall. The trolley wire shines above tracks laid on handmade basswood ties. The layout is so wired that power can come either from batteries or house current, and an old trolley car handle is the control switch—the kind of switch the motorman used to take off and carry with him when he left the car.

Captain Dosey manipulated the controller, and car #34 came alive and began to move at speed, past the stone crusher, along Big Fill to Gashouse Junction, through the tunnel into the Eastern Division, looping back again to the starting point.

The walls around the layout are painted with turn-of-the-century scenic views. I asked Captain Dosey whether he had painted them himself. He looked up from the intricate little trolley car he had created, clicking along on the track, its paintwork gleaming, its charming little seats inviting phantom passengers, its interior lights shining steadily behind period shades.

"Oh, no indeed!" he protested. "I'm no artist!"

Herbert Dosey, although his track was enhanced with "structures" and other scenic accessories, concentrated on the verisimilitude and perfection of the trolley cars he built. Blair Foulds is not concerned that his models be "scratch-built"; as long as the cars meet his exacting standards, he is willing to adapt ready-built cars, build from kits, or paint-finished, manufactured models along with building the trolleys

Five states are represented at this traction terminal on Blair Foulds's layout: Indiana, Illinois, Ohio, Pennsylvania, and Connecticut. Collection of Blair Foulds.

completely. His particular interest is in the number and kinds of trolley cars he can collect and run—an extremely impressive number, indeed, of captivating little cars, all of which he has painted and most of which he has hand-built to some degree.

Blair Foulds knows, along with most of his fellow enthusiasts, the history not only of the lines represented on his layout, but the history of many of the individual cars, and like many older hobbyists, he has ridden in a number of them. He likes to think up tours de force, such as pulling a string of freight cars that make up a traction train that includes a representative car from every line that interchanged freight cars with a steam railroad—a freight car so long that watching it run transports you in imagination to the driver's seat of an automobile halted at a grade crossing.

A modeler who concentrates on the *scene* surrounding his track is John Sheldon, of Yorktown Heights, New York. I saw some pictures of his trolleys in their habitat in *Traction Guidebook*, a handbook I picked up at a hobby store. I called him and arranged to come up and see his settings of Oneonta, a small town in upstate New York through which the Southern New York used to run, and which, the guide says, "lies deep in the hills at the western edge of the Catskills." In looking up the population of Oneonta (14,000 in 1969) I discovered that Oneonta was a particularly appropriate town to be immortalized in Mr. Sheldon's basement, for it was in Oneonta that the Brotherhood of Railroad Trainmen was formed in 1883.

John Sheldon has recreated Oneonta of the early 1920s. It is not a building-for-building replica with recognizable stores and churches, but rather a group of buildings so realistic and so much in the style of upstate New York of the period that you feel you've not only dropped back in time but, like Alice, have unaccountably "shut up like a telescope." The Southern New York Railway was an actual interurban that ran in a significant area of central New York State, from Oneonta

The hills and rocky terrain in this scene from John Sheldon's "Oneonta" neighborhood are typical of the land in that area. Collection of John Sheldon.

to Richfield Springs (also in Mr. Sheldon's layout) and towns like Cooperstown, where the Baseball Hall of Fame is, and that made connections or through runs to Utica.

John Sheldon's Oneonta has recently undergone an "urban renewal" program. "The city limits were expanded," he writes in the *Traction Guidebook*, "and new streets were laid." New track spurs were built "by the railroad" to serve industrial properties.

I do not want to give the impression that John Sheldon is someone so caught up in a world of make-believe that he has lost touch with reality. His approach to his little world of upstate New York is whimsical rather than hallucinatory. Among the industries that help support his Oneonta is a hosiery factory, which he has mischievously named the "Leatherstocking Hosiery Company." In his Richfield Springs there is "Hobson's Choice Variety Store," and Frank Schlegel again achieves notoriety in Mr. Sheldon's town of Hartwick, where there stands "Schlegel's Bagel Barn."

By stressing the structures and the scenery, I do not mean, either, to scant the Southern New York Railway in its incarnation here. There are two handsome interurban passenger cars on Sheldon's line, as well as box motors, locomotives, and powered maintenance equipment. He had written, "One also will find a Walkill Valley interurban roaming SNY rails as part of a joint service offered by SNY and the nearby Walkill Valley Traction Company." In mundane and colorless terms, he would say that the Walkill Valley Traction car belonging to a modeler friend is at this point running on Sheldon's layout.

But on this layout, more than on any other I have seen, the entire combination of cars, structures, accessories, and scenery work together to create illusion so strong and so joyful that it is no wonder Mr. Sheldon writes about his train system in such realistic terms.

He has set his towns—Oneonta, Richfield Springs, Hartwick—in a topography typical of the New York State countryside. Using a substance called "water putty," which outlasts plaster, on a base of wire mesh, he has created mountains and hills, rock cuts for the train to go through, and a variety of land surface matching the sharply rolling countryside of central New York State. His numerous trees are manufactured of real lichen, and come from England. There is a bridge on the line that Sheldon built after looking over one near his house that had been built for the virtually abandoned Putnam Division line of the New York Central Railroad. Sheldon's own bridge is a careful

A Southern New York trolley, a gas station, a winding road. An idyll of the recent past. Collection of John Sheldon.

replica, down to the tiny water barrel that sat next to the tracks as safety equipment.

John Sheldon first became interested in trolleys when, as a small boy living in New York City, his father took him along on a business trip upstate, and put young John on the interurban to ride while the elder Sheldon attended to his affairs. That was enough to inspire a devotion to trolley cars that John Sheldon has never lost.

For many years his interest was expressed only in a storing up of interurban knowledge. Then one day, on a commuter train to the city, he was spotted reading a railway magazine as he stood in the railfan's spot at the front window of the head car. The spotter was a member of the old Tappan Zee Model Railroad Club. Undeterred by the fact that the two men had never before laid eyes on one another, this hobbyist struck up a conversation with Sheldon and enlisted him in the model group. From this beginning, over a period of years, a move to Maine and back, and a summer spent near Oneonta, came the miniature

A Southern New York interurban car on a wood bridge between Hartwick and West Oneonta, over Tilley's Brook. This trestle has since been replaced in Sheldon's layout by one that is more elaborate and almost board for board and nail for nail a replica of a Putnam Valley Line (New York Central) trestle near Sheldon's house. Collection of John Sheldon.

world of 1920s Oneonta, Richfield Springs, Hartwick, and their surrounding countryside.

Sheldon makes some of his models by kit bashing, but that is really only the beginning for him. His old general store, for example, an ancient building just right for the cracker-barrel crowd, was sold in the model shops as a haunted house kit. Kit bashing in the hands of an artist, which Mr. Sheldon is, is merely a way to get the basic structure done easily so you can concentrate on the authenticating details. You use what you need from the kit and discard the rest. Sheldon built other structures in his layout from scratch, except for ready-made metal or plastic windows. In every instance, it is his visual imagination, his dexterity, his memory, and his sense of style that make his layout extraordinary.

The terrain, typical as it is of the area it represents, is dictated in its detail by the configurations of the Sheldon basement. It was necessary to build around the boiler, for instance, and the hilly landscape that obscures the house's fuse box is ingeniously divided so that a fuse can be changed when necessary. There are small touches everywhere: a tiny privy behind one building, little sheds for various purposes, a miniature sawhorse with a miniature saw leaning against it, HO people engaged in a variety of HO activities. As often happens in real life, an abandoned boxcar serves as a toolshed for the trolley line.

The Southern New York livery is trolley orange and tuscan red, with truck frames and undersides "industrial black," bright on the new cars, and, as Sheldon says, "as the equipment sees service, the orange darkens in color, and roofs and trim become more of a roof brown shade. Dust, mud, and rust show increasingly as signs of road duty on the industrial black. The road's veteran cars wear these badges of service with unspoken pride."

In a yard in Richfield Springs there is a small steam locomotive, performing only the function of adding to the scenery. It was made in Japan and, Sheldon's wife told me, "was so nice and shiny black when he got it. And right away, he smeared dirt and sand all over it, and made it look like this!" "This" is an engine that has seen much wear and could easily have been put out to pasture in its old age. It blends into the rest of the setting much more than it would with a satin-shiny finish straight from the paint shop.

I asked Mrs. Sheldon if she, too, was interested in model trolley lines, and she laughed. "After all these years," she said, "I've got to be." The club now is a social activity for its members as well as a strictly hobbyist group, and there are occasional parties and picnics where family members only marginally interested in model trolleys can enjoy the friendships they bring.

Mr. Sheldon ran his trolleys for me, and he, like Blair Foulds, runs them rather slowly, at about "scale speed." This means that they cover the HO equivalent of a mile at a speed that is related to the actual per mile speed by the same ratio. Both men commented that many hobbyists run their trains too fast, and that the illusion of reality is much stronger when they go at the proper speed. "Also," said Sheldon, "you can see them better."

In about 1940, Frank W. Schlegel made this beautiful model of Terre Haute, Indianapolis and Eastern car #37. It is entirely of brass, has truck frames built up of several pieces of metal, and careful detailing. Schlegel not only painted the car, but hand-lettered it. Photograph by Frank W. Schlegel. Collection of Blair Foulds.

He pointed out a spot to me where, if you crouch down a bit and look down the track through a rock cut, the scene is almost breathtakingly realistic and intensely delighting.

Different model makers will give you different reasons for their having gotten into the hobby; some of them don't really know what the reasons were, but simply say, "I wanted to do it." Frank Schlegel is an artist, and the interest he has in trolleys makes modeling them seem an almost inevitable way to express it. (Interestingly, Schlegel has no layout; he runs his extraordinarily beautiful cars on the layouts of friends.)

In talking to modelers, in reading all the unbelievably detailed hobby magazines, I realized what would be a strong basic motivation for me, were I to make models, and what I suspect motivates, at least in part, most model railroaders of all persuasions, if, unlike Schlegel, they do build layouts with their trains or trolley cars.

When you build a model railroad, you are doing more than just reproducing a complex object in miniature. You are creating an entire and complete world—a specific railway line, running in a specific landscape, on a specific route and schedule. Whether your backgrounds are elaborate paintings or simply a streak of blue sky, green trees, city skyline—whether you construct your own buildings or make them from snap-together kits, every item that is in the extensive area covered by your railroad must be reproduced. The villages you build are *your* villages and contain the buildings that *you* want to put in them. (As Blair Foulds said, "I put in an oil refinery because I like tank cars." If you like cattle cars, you can build ranches or packing houses, or both.)

You lay rail on the streets *you* want rail to be on and choose your paving material—brick, asphalt, blacktop—without concern for contractors or politicians. You are the lord of it all—the city planner, the mayor, the president of the railway—and who gives a fig for the ICC? Even Everett and Moore at the peak of their operations didn't have the power you have.

But "power" is the wrong word here—what creating a model layout gives you is "opportunity."

You've created this world, now. Set your cars to running and bring it all to life!

11
"Rails Alive '75"

A few years ago, Frank Schlegel wanted some truck frames—the flat metal piece that covers the wheels on the side of a trolley car. He made a pair by hand out of metal and took them to a professional metalworker. He, in turn, made molds and then cast several sets of frames, which Schlegel put on his own trolleys and generously distributed to his model-making friends.

Charley Sussman creates his cars from scratch. He uses wood, painstakingly building up window moldings, carving refinements to the roof line, painting embellishments by hand. But the metal wheel trucks and motors are beyond his competence; these he must buy from a model parts manufacturer.

John Wachinsky has a whole fleet of interurbans from the Lake Shore Electric Line that he created methodically from parts supplied by three different kit manufacturers. Wachinsky followed a *gestalt* approach—he felt that the whole result of his own creation was greater than the sum of the parts.

The cars of most model makers carry parts from a variety of sources. This is why standardization is important to the practice of scale modeling and why the National Model Railroad Association was formed in 1935. It was a way to unite the model makers into a pressure group that could compel manufacturers to follow set standards and therefore make interchangeable parts. Manufacturers who conform are awarded a commercially valuable document, the NMRA Certificate of Conformance, a citation every knowledgeable model maker looks for before buying.

Blair Foulds is on the Traction Standards Committee of the NMRA. He researched and furnished much of the data used in early issues of what is now Standard S6 of the club, and is the author of "Traction Plans Index," a bulletin published by the national group—a tremendous effort that was received by trolley modelers everywhere with much gratitude and satisfaction. He has done—and continues to do—experimental research on trolley standards, and modelers all over the country correspond with him about this work.

Foulds gives "clinics" at trolley meets around the country. He told me that standards exist on the size of the trolley wire, on just what the basic scale specifications are, and other critical aspects of the tiny cars. For not quite so important, but still desirable, dimensions, there are "Recommended Practices." The way you attach a trolley pole to the roof of a car, he confided, is a Recommended Practice, but he would like to make it a "Standard," so that he and his fellow model makers could be confident of being able to put a commercial trolley pole, for example, on a handmade car.

It was with this in mind, as well as other rather arcane aspects of his preoccupation, that Foulds was planning to go to the five-day NMRA convention in Dayton, Ohio, where the Traction Standards Committee would meet. I decided I would go to Dayton, too, and have a look at "Rails Alive '75," as the 1975 convention was named, and its constituency.

Dayton, Ohio, is a city of about 300,000 people, wide downtown streets ("so a horse and buggy could turn around in them" one young Daytonite told me), a large new convention hall dedicated to the native Wright Brothers, and a wonderfully efficient transit system featuring trolley buses. Sometimes called "trackless trolleys," these vehicles ride on rubber tires and look very much like the exhaust-belching Diesels and gasoline buses we all know. They are powered, however, like streetcars; the electricity on which they run comes from overhead wires, through trolley poles. (Trolley buses need two trolley poles on two overhead wires; a rail trolley car makes its ground connection through the contact of wheel with track, but trolley buses must have the extra wire instead.)

I arrived in Dayton on a hot August morning, and took a public van from the airport to the Convention Hall. The low, white building was shimmering in the sun, and delegates wearing blue badges swarmed in and out of the doors and along the streets and through the lobbies of Dayton's downtown motels and hotels where they were lodged. (Expecting something like 1,900 registrants, the convention signed up 2,707 before it was over.)

In spite of the unexpected crush of visitors, the affair was efficiently and smoothly managed—the result of what must have been long planning, since sites for the annual meeting are settled on three years in advance. Except for committee meetings, there were no business sessions; anyone who registered was a delegate.

This convention maintained the traditional hyperactivity of all such gatherings. The visitors came, most of them, in family units (a full and complex program of nonrailroading activity was provided for those spouses up to here with model trains). Not only model-makers' wives but model-makers' children thronged the Convention Hall, devouring pizza and hot dogs and Polish sausage sandwiches, haunting the operating railroad exhibits, and riding a little train that circled the perimeter of the exhibit area. There was no raucous night-on-the-town atmosphere, however, even though small bars were spotted in strategic places thoughout the hall. These were rather earnest, if jolly, people, out for a wholesome good time pursuing an absorbing avocation that most of them—and why not?—were slightly nutty about.

The organizers of the affair had arranged to shower serious model makers with a cornucopia of railfans' delights. Radiating from the Convention Hall itself (where there was a window from which you could watch the nearby railroad), trolley buses were chartered to carry NMRA members on "prototype trips" and "layout tours." In model hobby language, a "prototype" is the original object on which replicas are modeled. A prototype trip is a visit to the location where actual trains or trolleys can be seen. A layout tour is a trip to view track and scenery layouts—in this case to the homes of several of Dayton's native modelers. The list of layouts to be visited that was printed in the neat eighty-six-page convention "program and timetable" indicates how comparatively small the little band of trolley modelers is; of twenty-eight layouts open to view, only two were trolley scenes. However, a special trolley tour was scheduled for the next-to-last day of the convention, and that directed the fans to several more.

At the convention itself, there was a confusing variety of pleasures. Movie and slide shows, photograph exhibits, a "swap shop." From the length of the lines outside room 301 at any time, the activity taking place within, a "silent auction," was the most popular in all of Dayton. Sellers at the auction were any delegates who had model-related material to dispose of, either because they didn't want it or because they could turn an honest dollar on it. Buyers were—well, buyers! People looking for a bargain (which they only sometimes got), people looking to buy something they hadn't been able to find, and people just caught up in the excitement of beating out the competition.

In a silent auction, sellers offer their merchandise with a slip of paper next to each item on which is stipulated a minimum bid. Buyers write their bid on a sheet, and must increase each previous bid by a set minimum amount, here twenty-five cents up to a certain price and fifty cents after that. Ten percent of all sales went to the convention for their trouble, and they could have been giving away color television sets judging from the response.

It seemed odd to me that among the visitors to Dayton, it was almost a 100 percent masculine audience that was interested in the substance of "Rails Alive"; almost all the women were (quite literally) along for the ride. Although our society has always accepted the cliché that little *boys* are the ones interested in trains (and planes and automobiles), and little *girls* never get any farther along the march of transportation equipment than the horse or just possibly the sailboat, that is surely a myth, if a self-perpetuating one.

Model-making, however, can be an occupation so intricate, and the creation of the models' tiny world so enthralling, that it seems odd that women of NMRA for the most part were limited to subsidiary activities. Their only planned participation was a rather patronizing contest—for the best freight car from a kit, something that one would think any agile-fingered woman could create with one hand.

At the convention, a large "women's committee," made up of wives of the men whose committees had planned the main events, provided diversions for the "Railettes." While their men were watching trains, swapping models, visiting layouts, the women took in a bingo party, a fashion show, an "old-time" fashion show, a shopping trip. They went to see the Air Force Museum, Dayton's Carillon Park, the local amusement park, and an arts and crafts store, and spent a good part of one day on an antiques tour of some nearby towns.

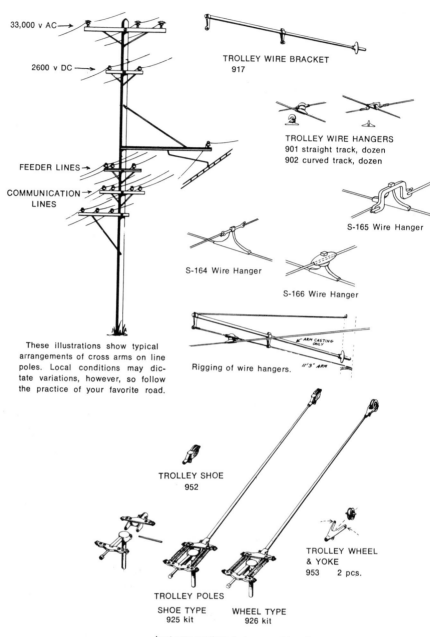

33,000 v AC→

2600 v DC →

FEEDER LINES →

COMMUNICATION →
LINES

TROLLEY WIRE BRACKET
917

TROLLEY WIRE HANGERS
901 straight track, dozen
902 curved track, dozen

S-165 Wire Hanger

S-164 Wire Hanger

S-166 Wire Hanger

These illustrations show typical arrangements of cross arms on line poles. Local conditions may dictate variations, however, so follow the practice of your favorite road.

Rigging of wire hangers.

TROLLEY SHOE
952

TROLLEY WHEEL
& YOKE
953   2 pcs.

TROLLEY POLES

SHOE TYPE   WHEEL TYPE
925 kit   926 kit

Lost-wax castings in brass and berylium copper. Full working, exquisite detail. Complete with springs and roof bushing. Exploded view shows assembly. Comes in kit form.

From catalogues of model trolley components come these appurtenances for stringing trolley wires. Reproduced from the catalogues of The Kemptron Corporation and E. Suydam & Co., Duarte, California, with their kind permission.

The husbands planned their time around clinics on subjects like "Track Planning," "Scratch-building Diesels from Styrene," "Heavy Industry and the Model Railroad"—eighteen different subjects (only one of them, though, having to do specifically with trolleys!). The Railettes, meanwhile, watched demonstrations of china painting, dog obedience, self-defense for women, silver jewelry-making, needlepoint, handcrafts (not including model-making), stained-glass objects of art, the contrivance of flowers from bread dough . . . and belly dancing.

Clinics are a feature of every model get-together. There it is possible to learn sophisticated tricks from the most experienced model makers. There one can benefit by a kind of group therapy effect: whatever your disability may be, whether it is being unable to connect the trolley pole springs effectively or having your car derail when it hits a complex switch, you are comforted to find that others have the same problem.

The one specifically traction clinic was called "Trackwork in Streets and Overhead Wire," and naturally, I attended it. It was given by Richard Orr, of whom the program said, "Dick Orr is a name well-known to the trolley and traction fellows." Dick Orr is a slight, dark man, by trade a printer, who carries in his bosom a gnawing wolf—that beast being the knowledge that the hardware commonly used to connect trolley wires and attach them to power poles and other supports is not in proper HO scale. It is larger; how significantly depends on one's personal standards, and Dick Orr's are high indeed.

At this two-hour session he was going to show us how he used some authentic HO hardware. Bear in mind that the pieces he objected to are about 5/16" long; his were smaller. Through these pieces of metal the wire—usually more than one wire—must be strung, secured, and soldered.

Nothing is simple. Orr began by laying tracks. A question that greatly exercises trolley modelers is how to transform "T" rail, used by the trunk railroads, into "girder rail," used in city streets by both street trolleys and interurbans. "T" rail is straightforward track; "girder rail" has an extra piece that acts as a wall to protect the wheel from the adjacent paving, particularly on curves. They have a choice of laying two rails close together, putting an extra piece of angled metal alongside the track, or doing as Dick Orr does. He sets another section of slightly smaller rail sideways, against the main track. Guidebooks will tell you that this is practical only on larger model layouts, like 0 gauge, but Orr intrepidly uses it on HO.

He laid a section of rail, spiked it to the composition baseboard, and proceeded, as we watched intently, to create brick paving around the new piece of trackage.

The interurbans almost always came into the towns they served, running either on the local street railway's tracks or on tracks of their own laid in the paved streets and conforming to local codes, so both streetcar and interurban modelers build streets. Brick was a widely used paving medium in trolley days, and adds a picturesque texture to a model layout. It is effective, and not especially difficult, to buy brick-embossed plastic or cardboard in a hobby shop, cut it to size, and glue it around your trolley tracks.

Premade brick, however, is not what Orr's models are all about. He creates his own brick paving from patching plaster. One of his tricks is to mix the dry patching plaster with dry tempera paint to get a kind of built-in color, more realistic than painting the color on after the street is laid.

Orr could have been preparing to eat a snack lunch instead of going about the creation of a brick street. His tools were a plastic spoon and cup, a soda straw, and a dull knife. The spoon and cup were for mixing the plaster, the soda straw allowed him to control the amount of water he was adding to it, and the knife was his tool for applying, smoothing, and marking the paving.

He had, in addition, a tiny homemade tool for cleaning the groove in his rail where the flange of the trolley wheel ran.

Orr smoothed the plaster, which was the consistency of peanut butter, around his rails and, with the dull knife, began to draw horizontal lines across it. He did it freehand; if the lines wavered slightly, so does a row of bricks. That done, he stabbed vertical lines into the plaster with the tip of his knife. Finally, Orr finished off the margin of the track area with a pattern familiar to anyone who has looked down at old-time streets—two rows of bricks laid perpendicular to the main section, forming a border.

Like the TV chef who has prepared four turkeys in different stages of doneness for his program, Orr had prepared a section of street the day before the clinic so as to have one that had dried the requisite time for the next step. With his knife, he attacked his careful brickwork, scraping away at it to give the edges of each brick a realistic worn look. He aged the reddish brickwork further by rubbing it hard with his finger, advising that you could use an oily rag if your finger wasn't dirty enough.

Now the wires. The audience was even more intent as Orr began planting double rows of power poles. The poles were of his own design and contrivance, and he had based the form of the tiny cap at the top of each on a long-abandoned but still standing trolley pole in his own city. (He had climbed out of an adjacent second-story window to lift off the cap so as to use it for reference. "They haven't noticed that it's missing," he told us.)

Each pair of poles was joined by a wire called a "cross span," and from these the electrical source, the contact wire, was strung. Everything was soldered into position with tiny drops of solder and a miniature "needlenose" soldering iron. There was an intricate spot where tracks branched off, or switched, and there were technical considerations to keep in mind. "When your tracks curve," Orr cautioned, "you have to run a car around them first and note where its trolley pole runs; it doesn't stay directly over the center of the track. You've got to use auxiliary wires to pull it into position." He told the intent listeners that NMRA traction standards committee chairman, Bruce Robinson, could furnish them with sets of calculations to help them do this.

Orr passed around his own HO "frogs," "ears," and "hangers," the miniscule pieces of hardware that were almost impossible to find again if one dropped them on the floor. He made working with them seem easy. When I said that to Blair Foulds later, he laughed and said, "I'm not so sure about that. I've seen him have some troubles himself with those small parts." Foulds had disagreed with Orr in the Traction Standards Committee session because Orr's small parts, he felt, were just too difficult for most modelers to handle. "We compromised," Foulds told me. That afternoon, however, all went well.

While the convention itself—clinics, Saturday night banquet, auction, layout tours—was sponsored by the National Model Railroad Association in its Dayton area branch, it was only half of the proceedings in Dayton that week.

The NMRA had the convention hall territory pretty well covered. Half the exhibit area was marked "delegates only." Here, among stands selling food and tables at which to eat it, there was a large oval track on which ran a train of miniature cars, each just big enough to

EMPORIUM, Limited

Scratchbuilders will delight in our fine line of detail molded plastic parts shown here. Most of these items are non-period and can be used on modern, old-western or victorian era buildings. All of these items are the finest in detail, workmanship and quality. They are all cast in white plastic with a few exceptions. Any of them can be used with the confidence that they will accentuate the beauty of your scratch-built structures.

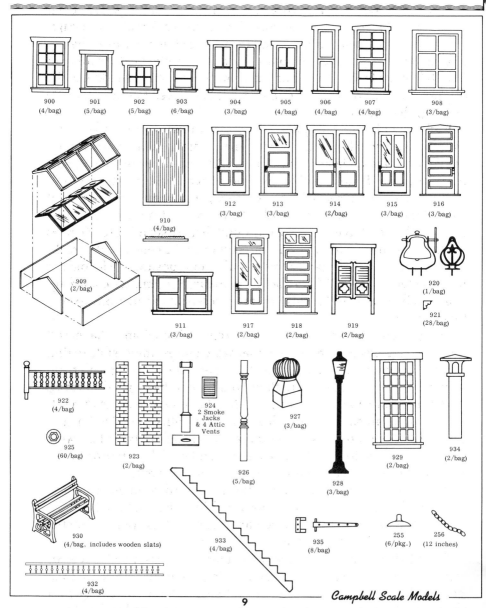

9

Campbell Scale Models

A small glimpse of the enormous stock of material specially made for model scenery/structure building: two pages from the catalogue of Campbell Scale Models. Courtesy of Campbell Scale Models, Tustin, California.

hold a giggling child or sheepish adult. The train was pulled by a locomotive belching real smoke; on occasion the hall became alarmingly cloudy. Then the speaker system would bellow, "The smoke is getting thick, so we're switching over to the interurban." And sure enough, the next time a mini-excursion came clacking by, the passengers were astride larger models of the Indiana Electric Railway.

The other half of the exhibit area, however, was the province of "MRIA," the Model Railway Industry Association. Here, there were rows of booths, where manufacturers and suppliers displayed their specialties. Touring the booths, I began to get some notion of the magnitude of this hobby that is a craft that is an industry.

Although the exhibits relevant to trolley modeling took most of my attention, some others were too astonishing to pass by. One of these was a booth featuring the Railroad Radio scanner, a device that you can buy—from $139 to $159—to put in your car or your home or to shuttle between the two. It will cut you into the conversation between railroad trains and their dispatchers. "Stick an antenna into the railroad's radio traffic," commanded their leaflet.

The publishers of *Model Railroader Magazine*, Kalmbach and Company, displayed their numerous books and other publications related to model railroading. A young woman there handed me a flyer, and I read, "Thoreau said, 'Many a man has dated a new era in his life from the reading of a book.' "

Once the new era has begun in the life of a fledgling model maker, he will find he can buy such luxuries as "walkaround throttles" for his layout (at $99.95 to $130.95) so that he will not be tied to one spot while operating his new trains and cars.

I found—and was enchanted with—small plastic bags filled with actual scale-sized coal in four forms: stoker, egg, lump, or dust. There were scale model wood chips and sawdust. There was, again in scale, earth, both regular and fine (and "fine" by HO standards is fine indeed!), there was white or brown sand, stone, iron ore, and regular or fine-textured grass in two different greens.

To make train operation more complex and thus more interesting, an enthusiast with enough money can install automatic couplers. These will hitch two cars together at a push. To separate them automatically, you simply stop them over a built-in magnetic uncoupling device in your track.

All up and down the aisles, "grain-of-wheat"-sized light bulbs, tiny light fixtures, and parts of fixtures winked on and off. To insure the

A good kit, a lot of patience, some skill, and here's what comes out. "Norm's Landing," a kit from Campbell Scale Models. This manufacturer makes most of his kits from prototypes and tells you that "Grandma's House" in the original is in Washington state and "still in grand repair." "Norm's Landing," however, is a "combination of calendar pictures, personal observation, and creative thinking." Photograph by Thomas J. Ayres, courtesy of Campbell Scale Models, Tustin, California.

proper lettering, insignia, and striping on model cars, two companies listed pages of decalcomanias for sale.

Model makers need an ambience for their trolleys or railroad trains. The scenery and structure part of the industry seemed thriving. It appeared that just about every fifth booth featured some kind of scenery in kits, "craftsman kits" (where the materials are supplied but must be cut and formed by the buyer), and finished pieces. The makers of one of the most enchanting lines of these products, Campbell Models, said daringly in their literature: "Small dioramas can be created with as much enjoyment with or without a railroad."

Suydam, a big traction model company on the West Coast that supplies trolley modelers with a tremendous variety of brass cars, sells structures and scenery as well. Their line includes an ice company with HO loading dock and scale 300-pound blocks of plastic ice (twelve cakes for fifty cents). But the feature of their convention display was a "Follies Theater" starring "Nelda the Nudist" and "20 Girls 20" with appropriate posters lining the portals. Who says model railroading is for kids?

At one booth, a young man sat putting together one of his company's craftsman kits—a model of a coal yard that is copied from an actual structure on the route of the Chesapeake & Ohio Railroad. Consisting of a frame house with a stone shed, the model is made of wood, with aluminum roofing and plastic stone siding. The kit furnishes plans, templates, and instructions, wood and aluminum siding, doors, windows, embossed plastic simulating stone. The instruction sheet has eighteen separate operations; having learned them by heart long before, the demonstrator worked from memory.

An enterprising manufacturer had brought to the display his stock of paperweights, plaques, and assorted objects, such as door knockers and house number frames reproduced from old railroad (and *one* trolley) car plates. A local artist sat drawing pen-and-ink renderings of old railroad cars and stations to sell.

If you prefer making your own structures, but stop somewhere short of molding brick or stone siding for the walls, you can buy this material at $2.10 for a piece a little larger than 9" x 7" and cut it yourself to whatever size you choose, as you can the corrugated aluminum that is sold for roofing. There are books of plans and drawings to guide you in your construction, and Gregg Glenwood Publishers has for sale a reprint of a charming book, originally intended for vacation homebuilders desiring a full-size house. Called *Palliser's Model Homes 1876*, it is a series of plans and drawings of Victorian frame houses, turreted, bayed, verandaed, nostalgic, from which the enterprising modeler can select a basis for his country retreat, haunted mansion, or converted rooming house.

One of the most engaging things about model trolley-making is that it carries built-in charm. If you are modeling airplanes, tanks, or even Diesel railroads, you either are not concerned with structures or, if you are, they will be relatively modern, and therefore relatively commonplace. But when you model trolleys you are most likely recreating the early days of this century, and your buildings reflect the slightly exotic quality it is possible to associate with the period. Many

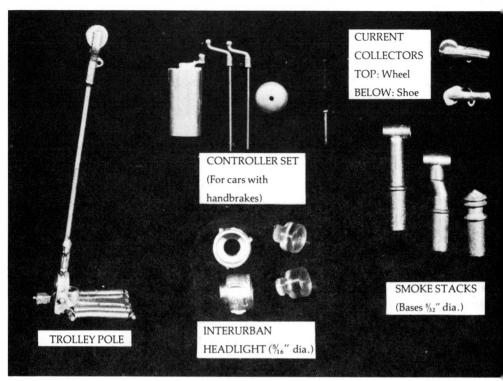

CURRENT
COLLECTORS
TOP: Wheel
BELOW: Shoe

CONTROLLER SET
(For cars with
handbrakes)

SMOKE STACKS
(Bases $\frac{5}{32}$" dia.)

TROLLEY POLE

INTERURBAN
HEADLIGHT ($\frac{5}{16}$" dia.)

Trolley parts, in scale, made for the modeler. Reproduced from the catalogue of Wagner Car Company, Wyoming, Ohio, with their kind permission.

of the miniature settings at the convention looked as though they came straight out of a movie—a Western or other period movie.

There were at least three working layouts on display at the NMRA in Dayton. One was billed as the largest N gauge layout in the world. It was strictly railroad; the tiny trains ran through a world that had never seen a trolley. But in another part of the hall a rail-modeling club in the Dayton area had set up a layout that was ecumenical.

Centered on their line, the "Cincinnati and Great Western," the layout had been designed so that it could be taken apart in sections that fit in the trunk of a standard American automobile. The club members, jointly responsible for the creation of what is an unusually intricate, realistic, and delightful layout, go from one house to another to work on it. They will even hire out with the layout for parties and other jollities.

The layout accommodates steam trains and trolley cars, both street and interurban. (The club member responsible for the handsome interurban station in this layout and probably a good deal more of the trolley work besides, later turned out to be the winner of the first prize for traction in the NMRA model contest.)

There were myriad business establishments in Clayton, the town on the Cincinnati and Great Western layout: beer distributors, a meat store, the inevitable lumber yard (there seems to be something about lumber yards that is irresistible to railroad and trolley modelers), a furniture factory, a barrel maker (whimsically called the "James Fenimore Cooperage"), the Wonder Water Heater Plant, a gas station, a box company. But it wasn't all business in Clayton; there were services, too: a fire department, a water tank and engine house, a coaling tower, the Clayton interurban passenger station scratch-built by award winner John Wissinger, a carbarn—I counted forty-one separate structures through which the steam passenger and freight trains puffed, with assertive recorded sound effects, and the interurban and street trolleys rolled.

On the other hand, the O gauge display contributed to the convention by the Indiana Museum of Transport and Communication at Noblesville, north of Indianapolis, had no scenery; it was impressive for its sheer size. Six parallel sets of track traversed a 306-foot

John W. Wissinger's HO scale model of a Pittsburgh Railways streetcar won the first prize for traction modeling at the Dayton Model Railroaders' convention. Photograph by Jim Hediger, courtesy of *Model Railroader* magazine.

oval. Two of the tracks carried overhead trolley wires, and running on five tracks were wonderful O scale models, presided over by the museum's Thomas Bader. There were medium-sized passenger trains pulled by steam or Diesel locomotives, and a freight train with two steam locomotives, pulling *ninety-seven* freight cars and faltering only occasionally and briefly. The final track seemed unoccupied, and since it was one with a trolley wire, I was concerned enough to question Mr. Bader about it. He looked surprised, checked back, and discovered that the lone Indiana Railroad Interurban had de-wired somewhere in the dim recesses at the far end of the layout.

When he had set the trolley back on the wire, the little interurban car quickly overtook and passed, in turn, the lumbering freight, and, one after another, the passenger trains. Could the steam roads be compared to the dinosaurs—too big to survive? Alas, they had had a longer and healthier life than the interurbans, even though they, too, succumbed in the end.

From the point of view of most convention visitors, the high point of the affair was the Saturday evening banquet. Tickets for this were part of the registration, and baby-sitting for the whole evening was laid on by the Women's Committee. Certainly every one of the 2,607 delegates must have been present in the jam-packed lobby for predinner drinks. The streets and Dayton DASH buses as the hour approached swirled with women in long skirts and careful new hairdos, and freshly shaven men wearing jackets and ties. (I saw nothing but short haircuts on the men, and very few mustaches or beards. The convention-goers were friendly middle-class middle-Americans for the most part; the hobby is not, as I have indicated, an inexpensive one and anyone who can afford to pay $199.95 for a locomotive for his basement layout is likely to be a pretty solid and conventional citizen. But the drinks session was as noisy and crowded as any Manhattan cocktail crush.)

I found Blair Foulds talking to a man from Toronto (Canada was well represented in Dayton) and we discussed my dream of traveling across Canada from coast to coast on the Canadian railroads. The Canadian gentleman advised me to do it while I could; he feared the trip's days were numbered. He also suggested that I fly to Calgary and start from there. "Before Calgary," he said, "it's a flat, stale, and unprofitable ride."

In the exhibit room the pizza and hot dog vendors had neatly transformed themselves into first-class caterers. Hundreds of round tables, covered with white cloths, centered with fresh flowers, awaited the diner. We all proceeded to take in a feast that must have been inspired by the memory of Diamond Jim Brady, the gourmand whose income from railroad speculation paid for his Lucullan meals. The main course, great chunks of very excellent roast beef, was almost dwarfed by first courses and vegetables, salads, pies, a stream of food. To feed all of those people and feed them so generously, was a major logistical feat.

Hobbyists from all over tenderly bring their models to the NMRA convention every year, hopefully submit them to the judges, and nervously await the Saturday night announcement of winners. It is honor, not profit, they are seeking; honor and a recognition of their considerable imagination and craftsmanship. There are no money prizes; the awards are ribbons, certificates, and satisfaction.

There were prizes for eight categories of model construction, including "Traction" and "Dioramas and Displays"; there were prizes for a number of categories of photography; and a prize award from the United Transportation Union called the "Brass Lantern Award." The NMRA gave a Gold Lantern Award to what they considered to be the very best model of all, and the magazine *Railroad Model Craftsman* gave a trophy to the model that "best captured the spirit of model railroading." It interested me that there was a separate contest for the design of a railroad pass; I later learned people use them for calling cards. There were prizes for locomotive performance and switching, for the best model by a woman (called a "Railette"—the woman, not the model), and the best model by a contestant under eighteen. This last was won by a young fellow of fifteen, who had built a really remarkable replica of a roundhouse, with three bays and a hinged roof that showed, when lifted, the huge cranes anchored in its ceiling that were used for raising engines. Everybody thanked everybody else, and then the entire convention sluggishly (because of the enormous dinner) adjourned to a series of rooms on the upper floor where the prize-winning models were on display. (You must realize that there were a large number of these. There were eight categories not including the special awards, and awards were given to the first three in each category, and then there were honorable mentions!)

I went up with the rest to see the models; I was most intrigued by the

Three views of the abandoned depression farmhouse, the model that won the Gold Award (Best in Show) for Jim Hopper, of Sarnia, Ontario, Canada. In HO scale, the buildings are about three inches high. Everything in the extensive scene was built from scratch, the structures put together board for board as a full-size house would have been. Walls were made up of exterior sheathing, studding, interior sheathing, wood lathes, and plaster. Hopper based the scene on a composite of an actual abandoned farmhouse he had observed. Photographs by Jim Hediger, courtesy of *Model Railroader* magazine.

scenic efforts, which were tiny worlds complete, like John Sheldon's layout at home, in every detail. I realized again that there is a lot more to the model train hobby than running trains around a track. The top prize of all, the Gold Lantern Award from the NMRA, was a farmhouse and its surrounding land. It was a farm that had fallen upon hard times, but that, of course, made the model that much more picturesque. The structures—the farm buildings of all sorts—were the kind of silver gray color that wood takes on when it hasn't been painted for many years, if ever. The land was sparse, but not as though the model maker hadn't put enough grass in, rather as though it hadn't rained in too long a while. Fences were sagging in spots, roof lines were slanted rather than straight, and the whole farm looked deserted and sad.

The prize-winning models were indeed ingenious, and included, along with a variety of scenery, cars far removed from the ordinary passenger or freight cars. There were old-fashioned balloon-style engines, and the most intricately detailed work cars and service cars. A very large percentage of the work was based on the vehicles of bygone days; very few model makers had been moved to create aluminum-skin skyscrapers or streamlined heavy electric commuter trains. They preferred split-log towns, prairie and mountain vistas, twenties-looking business enterprises. The mining companies showed as entrances to the shaft; strip mining has not yet hit the little world of model railroading. Unlike the child in Randall Jarrell's novel who wanted no doll for Christmas, but "a real baby with real wax in its ears," model railroaders seem quite content to recreate a romantic world of homey buildings and obsolete vehicles. And which of us wouldn't be?

There was dancing scheduled for the evening, and the band was warming up as I left the model display. But I took a trolley bus back to my motel went to bed, and dreamed of interurban trolleys going at ninety miles an hour in HO scale.

12
Museums That Move

There are life-sized interurban cars still running. In the everyday world, the Chicago, South Shore & South Bend carries passengers three times daily the ninety miles between the Indiana city and Chicago. (The line also operates a commuter service between Gary and Chicago.)

And that's it—the only honest-to-goodness interurban still operating The C,SS&SB has managed to hold on to it passenger service—as well as its life—by running a still profitable freight operation along its route. The income from that, tossed to the line's present master, the Chesapeake & Ohio Railroad, has so far kept the cost accountants at bay.

By looking around, however, you can still find—and ride in —the speedy, comfortable, wood or steel cars of the past. They roll on the tracks of the numerous trolley museums in North America. There are at least twenty working museums in this country and Canada devoted to or including trolleys, and many of these give rides in interurbans as well as street trolleys; just about every one of them has interurban cars on display. There are five or six major railroad museums in the country, too, most of which include interurban cars in their collections.

The word "museum" must be used in its broadest sense about the first group. Dana K. Bowers, one of the leading members of the Branford Electric Railway Association, which runs the trolley museum at Branford, Connecticut, said that as a teenager the word put him off for a long time.

The Chicago, South Shore & South Bend on a trip between the two cities. This is the only true interurban line still running on electric power and conforming to most of the characteristics of a true interurban. Photograph courtesy of Ron Brown.

Mr. Bowers is a slight, light-haired man in his late twenties or early thirties, pleasant and self assured. He is superintendent of operations at the Branford museum. "I'd spent a lot of time visiting my grandmother in Baltimore," he told me. "The Towson trolley line ran past her house, and I loved to ride the cars there; I spent most of my visits riding those cars."

But when, at home in Connecticut, his mother suggested he investigate the nearby trolley museum, he resisted. "*A museum!*" he said. "Who needed that? I didn't think much of the idea of going to see a lot of stuff in glass cases.

"Finally, one day, when it was hot and there was absolutely nothing my friend and I could think of to do, she started again. 'Go down and see what it's like, at least,' she told us. So we dragged ourselves over here. The first thing I saw was a trolley leaving for one of the trips, and that did it. Trolleys that ran! This was what a museum ought to be!" He shrugged and smiled. "I've been here ever since!"

The booklet put out by the Halston County Radial Railway, a trolley museum in Ontario (where "radial" is what they call inter-urbans) says, "The essence of transportation is *movement* . . . our museum is not a building full of old vehicles, preserved but dead; rather . . . a living railway in which visitors may ride." This principle of movement is true of all the trolley museums. Everyone has its mile or two—or more—of track and some operating cars.

They are, indeed, unusual institutions.

There is more to *any* substantial museum operation than meets the casual visitor's eye. While gangs of tourists tramp through the Museum of Natural History, examining the flora and fauna on view there, wondering at the ethnic handcrafts, the mock-ups of Maori canoeing scenes and the stuffed polar bears amid plastic ice floes, scientists in no-access parts of the building are planning expeditions, raising spider colonies, delving into various areas of the earth's life and landscape, and evaluating the results of previous forays into the field.

At a major art museum, restorers are at work, art historians use the facilities that are not open to the general public, experts verify the provenance of ancient paintings and sculpture.

These specialists are working at their professions.

At the trolley museums, the spankingly refurbished old trolleys and the delightful rides over their restored or scratch-built tracks are only surface evidence of what is essentially a heavy-industry operation done mostly by hand, with volunteer labor, at the minimum possible cost and in large part with hand tools.

All over the United States, and in Canada as well, there are groups of impassioned trolley fans who devote all their spare time, effort, and money to the loving restoration of derelict trolley cars, the upkeep of a section of track to run them on, and the barns to house them in.

Oddly enough, it was at the trolley museums that I saw the only women who were really active trolley hobbyists. I have heard of a few who build scenery and structures for their husbands' track layouts, but I never met one.

At Branford I saw several women wearing the uniform of a trolley crewperson, and operating trolleys in the pageant. I asked Frank Schlegel about it; he told me that there were a number of husband-and-wife teams, alternating as motorperson and conductor, and that the women had all trained on the trolleys for this purpose. When I

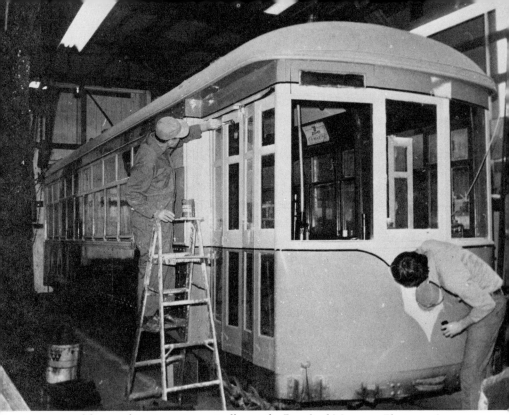

Men working to restore a trolley at the Branford Museum. Photograph courtesy of Frank W. Schlegel.

asked him if they all got into the hobby through their husbands, or whether there were some women who had become trolley enthusiasts independently, he smiled shyly.

"I met my wife up here," he said. "The first time I saw her she was training on #4573."

The future Mrs. Schlegel had been taken to the trolley museum by some friends, and had been so fired with enthusiasm that she came back and began to train to run the trolleys.

"We fellows were all standing around, waiting to make fun of her," he said. "But she did such a good job that when she brought the car back, we all applauded."

From this auspicious beginning the relationship blossomed. Schlegel was a widower; his first wife had died after a marriage of many years, and, he said, "I wasn't looking for a wife, or deciding that I should get married, or anything like that. But I came up here every weekend, and after awhile, we went out with another couple to a place around here—and it all just seemed to happen naturally. She hadn't been looking for a husband, either—although some of our friends kid her that she knew what she was doing when she came up here and started learning to run the cars!"

The first requirement of a trolley restoration project is the possession of a trolley car to restore. When one of the rapidly vanishing breeds of streetcar—and the almost entirely vanished interurban—becomes available, it is a real find, ramshackle though it may be. A trolley car that has been active up to the time the museum takes it is likely to be in better condition than one from some other source. But however dilapidated, any trolley car is usually considered to be better than none at all.

Whether the car itself must be bought or is donated, a large outlay of cash is necessary. You can't just attach a twenty- or twenty-five-ton trolley car to the back of your Chevrolet and tow it across the United States. (It is quite possible that when you take possession of the car, it doesn't even have any wheels.) It must be transported by railroad flatcar or flatbed truck, and has to be cumbersomely loaded on and off that vehicle. If the museum is lucky enough to be on a spur of a working railroad, the flatbed car bearing the prize can be switched over to its new home. But whether on railroad car or truck, the unloading process involves building a ramp from the bed to the trolley track, laying temporary rail on that ramp, and easing the car down. If you have acquired a wheelless shell, you'll have to unload it with a crane.

Although some cars are in reasonably good condition when the museum acquires them, many *are* only shells. They do not have the "trucks," so they are without not only wheels but motors and the frame to hold them. And without wheels you don't have brakes. They may be (and frequently are) seatless, with empty window frames and bare floors.

Though the members of the trolley museum association are clever, willing, and adept, they have neither the tools nor the equipment to manufacture these missing components; these must be searched out, and in their turn, purchased and transported. Paint, nails, tools, glue, every little thing that is used on or put into the car must be bought. It is not at all unusual for the members to dig into their own pockets to buy the necessary.

A museum garners cars from many different sources, in many different ways. If a line is going out of business and selling off its rolling stock, the word gets around quickly. Private owners may

A trolley museum can't ever have too many spare parts, since most of the cars they manage to acquire are bound to have missing wheels, or axles, or motors, or windows, or most of these, plus other parts.

Problem: How to transport a trolley when the tracks and wires have vanished. The Branford Museum gets a new car. Photographs courtesy of 35 Slides, Colorado Springs, Colorado.

Compared to some of the wrecks the museums bravely undertake to restore, the cars above and below are practically brand new! Photographs courtesy of 35 Slides, Colorado Springs, Colorado.

donate or will their precious trolleys to their favorite trolley museum. Occasionally someone unexpectedly finds that he or she owns a trolley car, and hastens to get rid of it, the way a city dweller will most generously hand over to a zoo the live grizzly bear his uncle had left him.

Smaller museums take anything they can get their hands on; larger ones that have been in existence for a while can afford to be more choosy, and to keep their function as custodians and historians of a past and future transportation medium more in mind. They buy (or otherwise acquire) with the goal of having a representative selection of trolleys, interurbans, and other equipment.

A common fantasy of railfans who haunt museums has all the drama of a TV thriller—and is realized much more often. That is the dream that the lucky enthusiast is speeding along through the countryside in his car, musing, perhaps, on where the relevant interurban line ran between the city he left that morning and the one he is approaching, when clang!

Was that a *trolley car?*

Business appointments and vacation reservations are forgotten. He stamps on the brakes and turns his car around, or looks impatiently for the next exit that will take him off the thruway.

Backtracking, he finds the spot again. Yes, it *is* a trolley car. Covered with vines, perhaps, or disguised as a milk house or a chicken coop, but a trolley car, unmistakably. And it seems to be—it looks like—it *is!*—from the street railway series 2000 double truck Birney, or the heavy combination interurban that once saw service along the shore of Lake Erie! Or some such.

He approaches the farmer on whose land this prize is so ignominiously sitting. The plot thickens. While the owner just may say, "Sure! Take it! I was going to tear it down anyhow," he could also turn out to be a suspicious type who immediately decides he has the equivalent of an unknown Blue Period Picasso and isn't going to let it go without what he considers due compensation. Alternatively, the encounter could produce a surly agriculturist who sets his dogs on the frustrated railfan before he can put in his bid for the soi-disant chicken house. (In which case, any *real* railfan will get on the phone and try a long-distance appeal; failing that, there are those, cynics say, who would make a note of the farmer's name and address and subscribe to the local paper so that the obituary column might alert them as to when they could approach the heirs.)

O. E. Carson didn't discover the object of his dreams in quite so dramatic a fashion, but subsequent events have certainly built into as thrilling a scenario in his case. And although his 40-odd-foot lovely is a city streetcar, not an interurban, his story so well illustrates the devotion and dedication of the trolley museum workers that I include it as a shining example.

I met Gene Carson on one of my trips to the Branford Electric Railway Association Museum; he was sitting in the motorman's section of an old trolley car in one of their carbarns, talking to a teenage trolley buff (yes, there are some of those, too) and carefully painting each one of a pile of metal seat brackets a rich red. He explained that these were destined "for 948." He spoke the number lovingly. (All trolley fans, I learned, refer to cars by their numbers, and the relationship between fan and trolley needn't be so intimate as Gene Carson's with 948 for the fan to know what number signifies which trolley. The numbers are not arbitrary—the cars were numbered by series, so that, for instance, car #65 on the Shaker Rapid is immediately recognizable as one that had originally been on the Indianapolis & Southern Railway, since all Shaker Heights cars at that time were given, when new, a different series of numbers.)

Talking to Carson, I soon discovered that he lives in Baltimore, but that he has been coming to Branford, a suburb of New Haven, Connecticut, every weekend for more than two years to work on 948.

"But there's a trolley museum in Baltimore!" I said in astonishment. "And one outside of Washington. Why come all this way?"

Car #948 was why. As a boy, Carson lived for a while in Atlanta, Georgia. In that southern city he conceived a devotion to the local streetcars that was to endure.

A few years ago, he got wind of the existence of three of the trolleys that had served the people of Atlanta until 1947, when the city converted its street railways to buses. At that time, Atlanta owned 200 trolley cars of the twenties vintage. Fifty of these were sold to the Republic of Korea, 30 for use in Seoul, 20 more for other towns and cities. (Railfans have information like this at the tips of their fingers, and it would be hard to restrain any really involved railfan who finds himself in say, Rangoon, from hopping over to Seoul to ride the old Atlanta streetcars.)

The remaining hundred and fifty Atlanta trolley cars were "cannibalized" to provide spare parts for the Koreans. Now here is the first, and least startling, of the series of what Carson calls "miracles" that has made it possible for him to realize his own trolley dream. At the time these cars were sold off, the price of scrap steel was very low. For that reason, the car bodies remaining in the United States, stripped of their working parts, escaped being sold for scrap—they weren't worth the trouble. Instead, various individual buyers took them to transform into summer cottages, diners, farm buildings, and the like.

Carson somehow learned that there were three of these Atlanta trolleys on the land of a farmer in the Georgia countryside, and determined to get hold of one. He immediately got in touch with their owner. Yes, he had three cars—well, really two, 948 and her sister 947. They were well preserved; he had them in a spot well away from the road. The third had been set down near the road and had been immediately vandalized to the point of unusability. (A 1970s touch, here.) And yes, he would sell one of the car bodies to Carson.

Hurrah! But what to do with it? A trolley car—one without any wheels, at that—was hardly something Carson could put in his front yard.

And now there took place the second of the chain of events that Carson only half-jokingly calls miracles. The Sunday following his conversation with the Georgia farmer, he picked up his local paper and read a story that described the Branford museum, calling it "the place where good trolleys go when they die."

Branford, of course, is only one of the trolley museums around the United States, but it is one of the oldest, best equipped, and has more than eighty trolleys and a large number of active members.

Branford it would be, then. Carson arranged to have 948 shipped to the only trolley museum he knew about—and that only because of a lucky browse through the Sunday supplement.

Eventually 948 was installed in one of the carbarns, and Carson began his weekly trek from Baltimore to East Haven. He leaves home on Friday after work, puts up at the houses of various hospitable BERA members in the area, devotes himself to 948 on Saturday and Sunday, and takes the train Sunday evening back to Baltimore.

Even before the arrival in Branford of 948, Gene Carson's own brand of miracle began showering down on him like sparks from an arcing trolley wire. (Of course, the fact that 948 had been completely stripped gave the miracles more scope—there were so many things she needed.)

It began when the car was being loaded onto the truck for transportation to Connecticut. One of the truckmen remarked that here was the second largest group of old Atlanta cars he'd seen. The largest was a flock that had been bought for farm outbuildings by Joe Bell, in Madison, Georgia.

Carson made for the nearest telephone and called Joe Bell.

Madison is the kind of town where the phone operator says "Joe? I think he went over to Henry Welch's. Let me try there." If he isn't at Henry's, she then remembers he said something about fixing a tractor tire, and rings the garage down the road.

Joe Bell was finally located visiting his brother-in-law. Yes, indeed, he had four cars. He was using them as the base of outbuildings on his farm. Why sure, Carson could come over and take a look at them.

When Carson arrived at Joe Bell's farm, Bell said, "Take anything you want. Just don't disturb the buildings." Carson's eyes widened when he saw how relatively well equipped Bell's cars were compared to 948. He left loaded down with colored glass for the upper windows, and an entire set of seat brackets.

Subsequently, trucks for 948 materialized in a forgotten corner of a Montreal carbarn—trucks identical to those on the Atlanta streetcars. "Imagine!" Carson said. "They'd been lying back there nobody knows how many years! And they turned up just in time for us!"

And if there is a patron saint of trolley cars, he—or she?—was rolling right on. No sooner had the Montreal trucks been delivered to Branford than the city of Philadelphia announced that it was scrapping some snow sweepers, which snow sweepers some of the BERA members just happened to know had brake rigging identical to the brake rigging used—on the Atlanta trolleys!

"Then, just as we were about to give up searching for the right kind of cork insulation, and use acoustic tile instead," Carson went on, "one of the members here went up to Hartford on business and heard about a big refrigeration tank they were taking apart up there. He thought he'd just go look it over. Well, there in that tank they used the same size cork that 948 needed for insulation. Not only the same size, and the same kind, but it had 'Armstrong' stamped across it just the way the original did."

So, as Fred Astaire once sang, "the day of miracles hadn't passed," although it helps to start a search for them with the outlook of an O. E. Carson.

Putting down his paintbrush, Gene Carson led me to another carbarn, and with all the false diffidence of a youth introducing his girl friend, he showed me 948. She is a handsome and well made car, a double truck trolley car with a deck roof. Carson told me that in the twenties Atlanta, like many other cities, had gone over to the dome

Pageant Day at the Branford Trolley Museum.
Photograph above courtesy of Frances G. Scott.

otograph above courtesy of
ances G. Scott.

roof, but the riders didn't like the change. They prevailed, and the company obligingly went back to the deck style.

The floors of 948 were covered wall to wall with heavy linoleum, her side panels were made of beautifully finished cherry wood with mahogany inlay, her fittings were of brass. Her doors, when open, did not protrude beyond the side of the car, as those of other trolleys did. "Too many drunk drivers came into town on Saturday nights," Gene Carson said. "Every time the trolley stopped, somebody would bash into the protruding door." The doors of 948 are on piano hinges and slide back into the wall of the car.

The outside wall of the trolley looks new and smooth, although it was broken when the car fell off the truck as it was being loaded in Georgia. "Luckily," Carson said, "it landed on the doorstep and that doorstep is part of the frame of the car, so we could fix it."

So, a step at a time, researching carefully all the way, in old records from the Georgia Power Company, in the memory of various trolley fans, in the annals of the *Street Railway Journal*, Carson, with the help of brother members of the Branford group, has been restoring 948 to the beauty that rode the streets of Atlanta. Walls, ceiling, all the wooden parts had to be scraped down to the bare wood, then painted and polished. Numerous components had to be mended; for others, substitutes had to be found—or, often, made, according to the specifications in old car company catalogues.

A final touch, one that finishes off all the passenger cars, will be the addition of the advertising car cards along the top of the long inner walls. There is a printer in the Midwest who produces replicas of period advertisements for restored trolleys.

Twice a year Branford holds a Pageant of Trolleys—a kind of trolley fashion show, when all the ambulatory cars are taken out and driven down the line for the delight of members and their families, other fans, and the usual complement of sightseeing visitors and their small fry. There is an accompaniment of knowing and good-natured commentary, and all the members come around, many of them in uniform, to run the cars. (Every trolley museum, I think, has something of the sort. At Rio Vista, in California, it is called Members Day, and elsewhere, under other names, similar celebrations of rolling stock take place.)

I made a point of getting to the spring pageant shortly after my visit with Gene Carson. It was a bright day, and the museum was far more crowded than usual. The women members—and the wives of men members—take it upon themselves on these occasions to set up a refreshment stand. They were dispensing hot dogs and soda, and at the side of the makeshift stand a washtub filled with water held ears of corn over a wood fire. Nearby, an ice cream truck did a rushing business.

There were familiar and unfamiliar faces under uniform caps. One elderly couple was wearing distinctive matching uniforms, which the wife told me she had made herself, "because we like to dress in uniform when we come up here." Children ran about and put pennies on the track for the cars to flatten, young parents pushed smaller offspring in strollers or carried them in their arms. There were cameras everywhere.

I encountered Carson again, in uniform this time, getting ready to take out one of the trolleys. He greeted me with what seems to be his habitual enthusiasm. "I'm not working on 948 today, but I will be tomorrow!" he cried. "But be sure to come up for the next pageant, in September. I hope I'll have 948 running by then! The electrical connections ought to be here in about ten days, and Jeff Norris will start putting them in. I don't do that part. I leave that to the experts.

"People say to me," he went on, " 'Gene, aren't you going to let down when 948 is running, after all this time?' Well, I'm not—not a bit. I've got two more cars lined up to work on. Don't just sit around brooding because you've finished one thing, that's what I say!"

The mix of people who find a mutual interest in working on and running the cars in a trolley museum is varied. To my surprise, most of the members are young, or young middle-aged. I did, however, meet the octogenarian Commander E. J. Quinby that day at Branford. The commander was dressed today in the striped coveralls of a railroad engineer, with the engineer's puffed and peaked cap and wide-cuffed gauntlets. He was preparing to pilot the museum's elegant Connecticut Company parlor car in the show.

The busy commander, of whom I had heard from Herman Rinke and who founded the Electric Railroaders' Association, is also the president of the corporation that runs the Mississippi riverboat *Delta Queen*, and his proud act had been to find, secure, and transport to the boat its calliope (pronounced, said Commander Quinby, "kaly-ope" if you're in the know). He had worked for awhile on a short-lived New Jersey light interurban line, and has written a delightful book about his experiences there. It is called *Interurban Interlude*, and includes reproductions of watercolors that Commander Quinby himself painted.

I met college students, railroad men, teachers, housewives, dentists, and commercial artists—all BERA members. A young man who had first come to Branford from his home in New Jersey to look at the prototype of a model trolley he was constructing came under the spell of the actual cars; he now commutes the considerable distance each weekend to work on them, and his younger brother has the models.

The teenager who had been with Gene Carson the day I met him is Joe Sweetman, called "Airtank" or just plain "Tank." A veteran trolley man at seventeen, Joe was given at an early age the responsibility of squeezing in between a newly arrived car and the carbarn wall and emptying the tanks of compressed air under the cars as a safety measure. "We old fellows," said the member who explained Joe's nickname to me, "tend to get pretty wide around the middle." So, like the little children employed in nineteenth-century coal mines to crawl through the narrowest tunnels pushing cars of coal, it became Joe's job to empty the tanks.

Many visitors are impelled, by their interest in transportation in general and trolleys in particular, to investigate the various cars on display at different stages of regeneration. The Seashore Trolley Museum in Kennebunkport, Maine, which owns the world's largest collection of electric street and railway vehicles, has a special gallery from which visitors can watch the restoration work being done. Seashore's collection of rolling stock is so extensive that a few years ago the city of Boston borrowed one of its emergency cars, and it is still in use there!

In most trolley museums, guests can actually ride the trolleys. Some groups were lucky enough to take over some of the trackage of a former trolley line or railroad. Trolleys can run on steam railroad tracks if both are of the conventional—and most widely used—gauge.

One, two, or several different cars, motor-manned and conducted by museum members, are operated continuously during museum hours for the delectation of visitors. A favorite type of car is the open, or "summer," streetcar, as they were called. The seats are rows of benches lined up behind one another from one end of the car to the

Showpiece of the Branford Trolley Museum, the elegant Connecticut Company officers' car. Officials of the line used it to travel over the entire system. Courtesy of Frank W. Schlegel.

other, and the conductor proceeds along a front-to-back running board as he collects fares. The car builders also made convertible cars; by removing the safety rails at the side, and fastening in removable side panels, the car converts from a "summer" to a "winter" trolley.

The 1½-mile track at Branford is like a scenic railway in that in a short distance it covers a varied terrain. The Branford trolley complex has the distinction of possessing a handsome station-cum-headquarters building donated by the widow and sons of Frank Julian Sprague, who was a native of the Branford area.

From the Sprague building, in what is essentially a suburban street, the track crosses the East Haven River on a trestle, rolls on through the carbarn area, past Farm River Road Station, a "country stop," to the Naragansett Siding, where the tracks from the carbarn join the main line in a tangle of overhead wire and ground-level rails and switches. Then it runs past the picnic grove, small descendant of the trolley parks, through woods and meadowland, around curves, over a hill, through a rock cut, past a quarry, and over a culvert that once accommodated the quarry cable railway on its way to the once-navigable river. The track emerges from the wood and goes over another trestle built of wooden piles, crosses a creek, traverses a salt marsh, and ends at Short Beach, a resort colony on Long Island Sound. It is a mini-interurban trip.

Originally, the track was double; one pair of rails for coming, one for going. But maintaining track is not easy; it takes constant work and constant dollar outlay. Reluctantly, the BERA tore up the second pair of rails and sold them and the ties to finance other projects. This sacrifice, in fact, made their line more authentically interurban; very few interurbans ran on double track. The only drawback at present is the absence of a loop at the end, so that the few cars owned by the museum that are not double-ended must be backed down the track after making a run.

The trolley tracks at Warehouse Point, farther north in Connecticut, go straight and level through fairly thick woods, and cross two paved, in-use roads on their route. The members of the Connecticut Electric Railway Association, which owns the museum, hope to be able to continue the line over the next stretch of terrain, which, with hills and dips and curves, is more challenging (if no more beautiful). Trolley cars can take steep grades and sharp curves with relative ease, and a hill that would cause engineering conferences on a

A small but charming part of the Connecticut Electric Trolley Museum.

railroad line (tunnel? climb? circumnavigate?) is equipped with rails and trolley wires without a second thought.

In Yakima, Washington, something rather special in the way of jolly trolley rides is going on. After a long search, the Convention and Visitors' Bureau of the city of Yakima, in the heart of the Washington fruit-growing country, found two trolley cars in Oporto, Portugal, that were identical to the ones the Yakima Valley Interurban had used from 1907 to 1929. They bought them, restored them, got permission from the Yakima Valley Transportation Company to use twenty-odd miles of their track if they kept out of the way of the YVT's freight trains, and are running lovely long trolley tours in the area. In Yakima you can go past fruit orchards, warehouses, and farmlands, over the Naches River on an old trestle bridge, or out to see one of the sights of the countryside, the eighty-room, native rock Congdon Castle.

The trolleys operate for the public on Saturday mornings and Sunday afternoons, and are available for two-hour charter excursions at various times. According to the sponsors, their "Trolleys, by Gollys," a Bicentennial project, is a wild success.

In Glenwood, Oregon, near Portland, there is a Trolley Park, run by the Oregon Electric Railway Historical Society. To get to the picnic

The popularity of "Trolleys by Golly" in Yakima, Washington, more than justifies the city's long search for the cars that ran in Yakima in the 1920s. They turned up in Lisbon, Portugal, and Yakima brought them home. Photograph courtesy of Yakima Interurban Trolley Lines.

grounds there, where there is fishing and swimming in a lovely lake, the daily visitors must ride one of the society's old trolley cars. On the way, they'll see a 1910-style trolley system, with shops, carbarn, depot, and numerous cars. You can ride in a double-decker streetcar from Blackpool, England, an open car from Sydney, Australia, or, at times, in their one interurban, a British Columbia car.

The Bay Area Electric Railroad Association started collecting their cars after the Sacramento Northern Railway gave up passenger service. The founders were all rail enthusiasts who for years rode that line every Sunday morning. The group enthusiastically collected a number of cars, but for fourteen years they neglected to find a place to put them, and the cars were stored with accommodating operating railroads. Finally, Bay Area ERA bought twenty-three acres in Rio Vista Junction, California. There, in Solano County, halfway between San Francisco and Sacramento, they built a large carbarn and more than two miles of track, gathered their trolley cars, and started rolling. Occasional special members' trips follow a longer route; the Sacramento Northern provides tracks, and, in place of trolley wire, a Diesel locomotive for power.

For trolley fans involved in the restoration of old cars, patience is not a virtue but a necessity. Bay Area ERA has two cars on the way to new life right now. They have air brakes, the bodies are mounted on trucks, but the electrical gear hasn't yet been put together, and so the cars are not operable. Work is progressing, however, and an optimistic letter from Addison Leflin, Jr., the group's secretary, says, "We hope to see the Petaluma and Santa Rosa #63 running as a regular

Salt Lake and Utah observation car, coupled to Sacramento Northern combination (passenger and baggage) car #1005 at Rio Vista Junction. The track in the foreground is the former Montezuma Branch of the Sacramento Northern. Photograph by Addison H. Laflin, Jr.

interurban motor car sometime in the year after next." When you are doing handwork on a piece of heavy machinery, you take the long view.

Most of the museums have at least one interurban car, and many of them are run for riders. If you use a broader definition of "interurban," you can ride them in California, Illinois, Indiana, Ohio, Pennsylvania, Washington, and Ontario, Canada. You can *see* them all over the place. (There is a listing of trolley museums on pages 201–213.)

Restoring and running cars are not the only jobs at a trolley museum. Some members maintain track, lay new ties and rails, and install overhead wire. At a busy museum, those who operate the cars include not only "motorpersons" and conductors, but superintendents of operation and dispatchers. And make no mistake about it, these people really work. They don't just do it for the fun of donning a uniform and playing at trolley cars. Taking the public for rides is a major source of much-needed revenue, and these members put in long days of labor standing in the sun issuing dispatching instructions, looking into minor derailments, and so forth. With many, it is a full-time part-time occupation.

Someone has to man (or usually, *woman*) the gift shops, presiding at the counter, selecting and buying the merchandise, arranging the cases of trolley motif key rings, books, pamphlets, photographs, postcards, with perhaps a stuffed bunny or two in addition. The gift shop wares range from ceramic insulators and other trolley artifacts —destination signs, lanterns, etc.—to manufactured objects, such as toy streetcars, model kits, tie tacks, and specially made bookends, plaques, and cigarette boxes laminated with colored pictures of the museum's own trolleys. The stock even includes, in some places, those wisecracking plaques with bucolic off-color jokes that people nail up on the walls of their basement recreation rooms.

Other volunteers handle the static displays, which vary. Branford has a small museum of models and photographs in the Sprague building. The Connecticut Electric Railway Association at Warehouse Point, on the other hand, owns fifteen one-inch-to-the-foot model cars, which it has no place to show. The Indiana Museum of Transport and Communication runs a large research library, in addition to a display of interurban fixtures, paper, and photographs, and the large operating model layout that I saw at the NMRA convention.

Every little bit helps.

With ties costing ten to twelve dollars apiece, and track spikes at forty-five dollars a keg, this is no nickel-and-dime enterprise. The job of raising money devolves upon those select and energetic members whose special talent that is. Grants, private donations from individuals and firms, special events such as trolley tours, and the admission and riding charges the public pays are all ways of securing the staggering sums that the maintenance of such a museum takes. Proceeds from the gift shop, of course, also swell the kitty.

Behind the scenes, along with the money-raisers, are various other administrative wallahs, doing various other administrative jobs. Writers, usually of some talent, fashion the brochures and striking color booklets that deal with the museum itself. Bookkeeping-accounting people keep track of the cash and pay the bills.

Photography is an integral part of trolley enthusiasm; the one way to record transitory phenomena. It is also a convenient way to keep trolley cars in your desk drawer. The museum's official photographer is a busy person.

One of Gerald Brookings's beautifully restored Interurbans at Trolleyville, U.S.A., in Olmsted Falls, Ohio.

Finally, there are those who also serve by standing and waiting and paying their dues, the members whose activity is limited to an occasional visit and an important yearly check.

An exception to all this—and the only one of its kind that I know of—is "Trolleyville, U.S.A." in Olmsted Falls, Ohio, just outside Cleveland. This is the private enterprise of Gerald Brookings, a long-time ERA member. In a shopping center he owns there, he has installed a carbarn with beautifully, professionally restored trolley cars, which he operates for the public. But the majority of trolley museums are staffed and financed by volunteers.

All sorts of people visit the trolley museums—the older ones have come in search of nostalgia and, believe me, they find it. It is indeed nostalgic, on a hot July day, to trundle through the woods in an open trolley, with a perspiring middle-aged or elderly man in uniform at the controller and a younger one making his way down the running board, punching tickets and ringing them up on the Ohmer register. The wheels make a gentle clack on the rails in the still, hot air, leaves from the trees along the track swish against the roof supports—we are in the country, we are in the last century.

Young couples have brought their children, who seem almost universally to love the ride—only the very youngest fuss and that only when the car stops.

During the summer, buses continually disgorge loads of small campers or even smaller day campers, with their amused and harried counselors. Senior citizens arrive, a gaggle of Scouts, the members of a historical society, motorcycle clubs, which roar up and docilely park their modern transport while they ride the older kind. Antique car buffs in vehicular parade stop off for a trolley ride, their Model Ts and Hupmobiles looking quite in place in the museum's parking lot. Schools bring chattering classrooms full of kids for a real-life lesson in economic history, geography, Americana. Church groups arrive in jolly bus loads of modern theological enterprise. And state and interstate highway commissions, unafraid of potential competition, provide signs by the side of the thruways directing tourists to the trolley museum.

And so the trolleys are running—life-size, under their own power, on their own private track, strictly for the delight of thousands of Americans every month. Off in the distance the faintest of rumblings (some of it in underground oil wells) indicates the slim possibility that the trolleys will be running on business, too, some day rather soon—the business of taking people not just for a mile or so through the countryside, but from one place in the real world to another.

13
Is Anything Coming?

In the 1880s a means had to be found for getting about the coun-tryside—a means that was inexpensive, was more convenient to a dispersed population than trains, was faster, and had more endurance than a horse and wagon. History and technology were obliging in this instance, and the interurbans met these needs.

The problem is with us again: how to go intermediate distances with reasonable speed, at reasonable cost, treating the environment with respect, and spending fossil fuels penuriously.

The distinction that used to obtain between urban, suburban, and midrange interurban travel has disappeared; many of the same dif-ficulties plague all of them and many possible solutions would be effective when applied to a trip uptown, a commute to the suburbs, or a business call to a nearby city.

Atlantic Richfield, an oil company with a daring public relations adviser, ran ads awhile back asking the public to contribute their ideas on mass transportation. Many of the 30,000 suggestions they received are as applicable to travel between cities as within metropolitan areas.

When 600 transit planners met in Philadelphia recently to discuss light rail transit, a new, highfalutin' name for trolley cars, they specifically spoke about transportation within cities and their im-mediate suburbs. But it would not require much modification of any of their statements and conclusions to arrive at a modern interurban system that could supplement the airlines and the heavy rail transport that now exists and remove a significant number of private automobiles and buses from the roads.

One of the arguments against building a rail network is its inflexibility, an argument which ignores the fact that a six-lane highway isn't very easy to move, either. But the inflexibility of rail travel is just one of the minuses that must be balanced against the plus factors, and the latter are beginning to take on increasing weight.

The state of Connecticut for the past few years has had an imaginative transportation program. One phase of it is the acquisition of disused railroad rights-of-way for possible future use. At this writing, Connecticut has acquired 200 miles of abandoned track (at a very low cost), and is waiting to pounce on any other that becomes available. "Once it is cut up and sold," the commissioner of transportation, Samuel Kanell, says, "that's it. If you had to put it together again, the cost would be prohibitive." The time is past when a few shares of stock and the promise of a stop on the property secured right-of-way over several hundred acres.

Connecticut calls its track, collectively, the Temporary Land Bank, and it is not letting it all lie idle. The land has become bicycle trails, hiking trails, the site of a steam excursion train, and just plain greenbelt. The total investment is very low; some land is donated by its owners or directors. The state, says the manual the department has put out outlining the transportation plan, is actively attempting to purchase all such privately owned rail transports. They could be used eventually for revivified railroads. They could also be used, it seems, for an operation such as the Lindenwold Line in New Jersey, which has been instituted by the Port Authority Transit (PATCO) to coordinate service with the Transport of New Jersey and Dial-a-Ride buses near Philadelphia.

The line (in whose electrical design, incidentally, that same Jeff Norris, who helps install the electricity in Branford's restored trolley cars, was very much involved) has been operating with great success over a fourteen-mile section of track from Camden to Lindenwold, with extensions planned. It is an electric suburban line; one that might be called a modern descendant of an interurban.

As this is being written, 175 modern trolley cars are on order from Boeing Vertol Corporation for the city of Boston and its adjacent suburbs, and 100 more are being made for San Francisco to supplement the present trolleys, the cable cars, and the BART. Pittsburgh, Newark, Shaker Heights, New Orleans, and Philadelphia have functioning trolley lines that suddenly seem—to planners and public—strangely beautiful. Dayton, Ohio, and Rochester, New

The trolley of the present—the Boeing Vertol Light Rail Vehicle (the LRV). Photograph courtesy of Boeing Vertol Company.

York, are planning new lines. In the end, it is the public who must accept any transit system that is to be successful, and there was tremendous public interest in the Philadelphia conference. Newspaper stories, interviews, and reprints of the Toonerville Trolley cartoons bobbed up in the wake of the conference, and the return of the trolley is becoming a conversation piece even among those who have never seen one in their lives.

Two up-to-the-minute cars have been developed and built in prototype; one, the "State of the Art" car (SOAC) is what the U.S. Department of Transportation is presenting now as a model of the possible. It demonstrates the optimum in current technology, and the designers set out to make an extra quiet, vandalproof, speedy car.

At the same time, the U.S. Department of Transportation dangles before us the car of the future. The ACT-1 (Advanced Concept Train) will be even quieter, faster, smoother, with better acceleration, more glorious decor, and more riding comfort. A third car is the reality, the car Boston and San Francisco have ordered and expect to be able to afford, the LRV, the Boeing Vertol Light Rail Vehicle, which is no slouch itself. In a paper presented at the Philadelphia conference, Joseph S. Silien, the director of the U.S. Office of Transportation's

The Electric Economy. A good idea whose time has come–again.

This ad appeared in the summer of 1975 in *The New York Times* and other newspapers in the United States. Reproduced courtesy of The Southern Company, Atlanta, Georgia.

Rail Technology Division, and Jeffrey J. G. Mora, the rail transportation projects manager, very specifically invoke Dr. Thomas Conway's PCC, the Presidents' Conference Car of 1933, implying that the same vision that beckoned Conway glows in the darkness ahead of them—trolley lines operating efficiently, speedily, and profitably. Or, anyhow, breaking even!

When it became possible for an ordinary man to buy an automobile, the existing alternatives—the passenger steam roads and the interurban trolleys—were active enough to keep highways clear of excess traffic and make driving a pleasure. (If a motorist had mechanical trouble with his new car, or ran out of gas, there was usually a trolley stop somewhere nearby to connect him with a distant mechanic or filling station.) Now that automobiles and roads have multiplied to the point where motor travel is a distasteful and often dangerous undertaking, many believe that it is time for some modernized version of the interurban to relieve the crush on the roads and help us cover intermediate distances with safety and dispatch.

In 1890, the farmer twenty-five miles from town had a problem bringing his produce to market; the steam railway wasn't available for trips of that distance, the horse took so long to arrive in town that the vegetables he carried wilted in the summer heat.

In the 1970s the farmer has his own pickup truck. It has more stamina than the horse, but it costs more to "feed," its exhalations pollute the atmosphere, and, if the traffic is heavy, he may still arrive with wilted vegetables.

It is time for another alternative.

"New interurbans" would have to find either crossing-free rights-of-way or plan to operate above or below the ground. Although BART in the San Francisco area has disappointed many, it has at the very least provided an object lesson for future projects, and there is no reason to believe that its problems cannot be solved.

Many believe it is anachronistic to build an elevated line that will only depreciate the residential and business areas through which it passes. For the same reason, a monorail is contrary to the trend of city planning, which is to eliminate overhead obstructions. The Seattle World's Fair monorail takes up a whole city street.

When new superhighways are planned, there are groups who try to have them include a median strip for some kind of mass transportation—interurban freeways incorporating interurban railways.

When the interurbans were abandoning their rights-of-way, Herbert Dosey became a one-man propaganda machine, addressing civic groups and commercial gatherings, urging that the franchises be retained for the benefit of the public. Jim Businger has visions of a fleet of buses, possibly powered by Diesel electric motors, that would run on slots in the inner city streets, or on some sort of track. They would go from the central city in trains through an underground tunnel. When they reached suburban or residential areas, the train would split up into individual buses that could be driven like ordinary motor buses on the street.

The Harlem Division of the New York Central Railroad runs commuter trains the fifty-two miles between Grand Central Station and Brewster, New York, and maintains a thirty-mile-per-hour average in spite of several stops and the mandatory slowdown in the Park Avenue tunnel. Almost all grade crossings have been eliminated from this line. Some students of the transit problem recommend that the Harlem Division be modernized to the point where the remaining grade crossings are eliminated and an average speed of forty miles an hour scheduled. Were this to be accomplished, the line well could serve, they feel, as a model for new transport.

It is true that the interurbans failed, but the two factors that caused their failure would not operate in a modern version. They failed because of the fight put up by the automobile companies, but since mass transit is now urgent precisely because the land is overpopulated with automobiles, restoring decent rail service would help both the rail traveler and the motorist.

The interurbans failed, too, because they returned such a low rate on investment; even when business was good, operating costs were too high to make it profitable. But no one now expects mass transit to be self-supporting. Automobiles enjoy a government subsidy in the form of free or low-toll roads. Public transportation can, of course, enjoy similar benefits.

If any of the proposals for intermediate-distance travel can be realized with reasonable success, if the railroads concentrate on hauls too short for jet planes and too long for rapid transit, we may once again have a system of transportation that meets different human needs at different speeds.

It is doubtful that whatever materializes to augment the motorcar will provide the same amenities as the interurban trolleys did. It is unlikely that conductors will go back to doing homely errands for housewives along their route, that lovers will consider a transit ride delightful entertainment for a summer night's date, or that motormen will wait and whistle for a rider who is late. (In fact, it is unlikely that motormen and conductors, as such, will exist much longer.) But perhaps the new transport will arrange amenities of its own. Its proponents hope that it will make at least one major change: that the trains will operate through the countryside at a level of speed, convenience, cleanliness, and comfort that will make travel between cities and towns a pleasure once more.

Trolley Museums
and Related Attractions

Note: Hours, admission prices, and possibly other aspects of these listings may change. It would be wise to phone or write ahead to check open dates and times, or else get up-to-date information from a local tourist bureau.

Most of the regular museums will arrange charter service for large groups and parties, but they need advance notice.

In almost all museums, very young children (under six or under four) are admitted free. Charges usually are made for rides; admission is usually free.

This listing may possibly miss some museums. We ask not only forgiveness, but a letter to correct future editions.

CALIFORNIA

Travel Town
Department of Recreation and Parks
Griffith Park, Los Angeles, CA 90027
(213) 662-5874

Directions: Take the Ventura Freeway, turn off at the Forest Lawn Drive exit, and go east a short distance to Griffith Park and the museum.

Open: Every day, year round, 9 A.M. to 5 P.M.

Rates: No admission charge. Rides $.35 for adults, $.25 for children.

Features: Trolley ride in a gasoline-powered Los Angeles streetcar, on a track one-half mile long.

Other amenities: Planes, steam trains, fire trucks, and old automobiles. Refreshments, picnic area.

Orange Empire Railway Museum
P.O. Box 548, Perris, CA 92370
(714) 657-2605

Directions: The museum is on U.S. 395, seventeen miles south of Riverside, in the city of Perris. From Los Angeles take I-10 and California 60 to Riverside, then U.S. 395

Trolleys

going south. From San Diego go north on U.S. 395 to the museum. Perris is eighty-five miles southeast of Los Angeles.

Open: Daily except Thanksgiving and Christmas, 9 A.M. to dark; in summer until 6 P.M. Streetcars run Saturdays, Sundays, and most holidays, 11:30 A.M. to 5:30 P.M.

Rates: Adults $1.00 ($2.00 for all day), children $.50 and $1.00.

Features: The museum operates its trolleys on *two* tracks: one on a line passing the museum, the other on a loop ride around the edge of the grounds. Orange Empire owns several interurbans in various stages of restoration and runs them occasionally; but at this time and until the latter are fully restored, the museum is running city and suburban-type streetcars.

Orange Empire is one of the largest of the trolley museums. They have a roster of nearly eighty cars, including eight interurbans. Almost all their rolling stock is from West Coast lines—Pacific Electric, Los Angeles Railway, San Diego & Arizona, Fresno Traction, and a Los Angeles Railway funeral car, *Descanso* (which means "rest"). There is, as a change from the U.S. West Coast stock, a double-decker trolley car from Ireland.

Other amenities: A gable-roofed depot, railroad cars containing exhibits of railroad and trolleyana, a gift shop and old store, and a picnic area. Campers are welcome in the outer parking lot.

CALIFORNIA RAILWAY MUSEUM, Rio Vista
(Run by the Bay Area Electric Railroad Association)
2119 Marin Avenue
Berkeley, CA 94707
(707) 374-2978

Directions: The museum is on State Rte 12, halfway between Fairfield and Rio Vista, where State Highway 12 passes over the Sacramento Northern track. From San Francisco and Oakland, take I-80 to Fairfield turnoff, and State Rte 12 to Rio Vista.

Open: Saturday and Sunday afternoons, year round, noon to 5 P.M.

Rates: Adults $1.00, children $.50 for unlimited rides on the day of sale. No admission charge to the museum.

Features: Bay Area runs its rolling stock on about one-and-a-half miles of track. The museum owns a unique piece of equipment: a portable substation, the only one on display in any electric railway museum. It is used to power the operating trolleys.

A large proportion of Bay Area's equipment is in interurban cars. There are two Southern Pacific (Interurban Electric Railway) line cars—a motorized passenger car and a passenger trailer; two Sacramento Northern cars and one from the Salt Lake & Utah Railroad; a Cedar Rapids & Iowa City Railway car, which originally belonged to the Cincinnati & Lake Erie and has been alternately a trailer and a motorized car. There are also Central California Traction #7 (once Washington, Baltimore & Annapolis #1), two Peninsular Railway small interurban passenger cars, and, finally, two articulated Key System cars, which were in the line that traveled over the San Francisco–Oakland Bay Bridge.

Other amenities: Refreshments, gift shop, picnic area.

202

COLORADO

COLORADO RAILROAD MUSEUM
P.O. Box 10
Golden, CO 80401
(303) 279-4591

Directions: Golden is a few miles west of Denver. Take I-70 to exit 64.

Open: Daily, year round, 9 A.M. to 5 P.M.

Rates: Adults $1.25, children $.50.

Features: Occasionally a steam locomotive travels in the museum grounds on a Saturday or Sunday, but the displays, which include a few trolley cars, are very largely stationary.

CONNECTICUT

BRANFORD ELECTRIC RAILWAY, East Haven
(Run by the Branford Electric Railway Association)
Branford Trolley Museum
17 River Street
Branford, CT 06405
(203) 469-9627

Directions: Take the Connecticut Turnpike (95) to exit 51 if eastbound, 52 if westbound. Follow signs to the trolley museum.

Open: Daily, June 23 to Labor Day; weekends and holiday, May 26 to June 23 and Labor Day to October 31. Open Sundays only in April, first three weeks in May, and all of November. 10 A.M. to 5 P.M. weekdays, 11 A.M. to 6 P.M. weekends.

Rates: Adults $1.50, children $.75. Unlimited rides on the day of purchase.

Features: You'll not only get the lovely three-mile Branford ride here, in an open and/or closed trolley car, but you'll get as well a guided tour through the carbarns, where you'll find, among the eighty or so pieces of trolley equipment, North Shore Interurban #709 (which is sometimes operated on rides), a Cincinnati & Lake Erie lightweight car, and Montreal & Southern Counties #9—interurbans all. Don't miss #500, the parlor car that used to transport officials of the Connecticut Company over the line on inspection trips. It has the original wicker furniture with plush cushions, carpeting, and a patterned floor. There are numerous varied work cars, some from rapid transit lines such as the New York City subway system.

Other amenities: Gift shop, picnic grounds, special days (call the museum for dates).

WAREHOUSE POINT TROLLEY MUSEUM
(Run by the Connecticut Electric Railway Association)
P.O. Box 436
Warehouse Point, CT 06088
(203) 623-7417

Directions: The museum is on Rte 140, north of Hartford, half a mile east of the Bridge Street exit of I-91.

Trolleys

Open: July 1 through Labor Day, every day but Monday; Saturdays, Sundays, and holidays only March through the end of June, and Labor Day through the end of December; closed Christmas; Sundays only the remainder of the year. Trolleys operate 10 A.M. to 3 P.M. in summer, 1 P.M. to 5 P.M. spring and fall.

Rates: Admission to grounds is free. Rides, adults $1.00, children $.50.

Features: The trolley travels a three-miles round trip through heavily wooded land with clearings where some of the work is done and some of the cars are stored. The line crosses a traveled road, slowing down to look and listen before sailing across.

The more than forty pieces of equipment at Warehouse Point include Illinois Terminal car #451 and the fabulous Montreal observation car, with its stepped seats and arches bearing bare light bulbs.

Other amenities: Gift shop, fire engine museum on the premises, picnic area.

DISTRICT OF COLUMBIA
(See Bethesda, Maryland)

ILLINOIS

R.E.L.I.C./THE FOX RIVER LINE
R.E.L.I.C. Trolley Museum
P.O. Box 752
South Elgin, IL 60177
(312) 697-4676

Directions: From Chicago, take I-90 northwest. Exit at Elgin and go south on Rte 31 to the trolley line's Castlemuir Depot, not far from the Interstate.

Open: Sundays and holidays through the end of October. Cars run 11 A.M. to 6 P.M.

Rates: Adults $1.00, two rides for $1.50; children $.50 and $.75.

Features: The two-and-a-half-mile round trip the trolley takes along the Fox River is a lovely ride. The trackage was once the property of the Aurora, Elgin & Fox River line, an interurban.

R.E.L.I.C. has a number of interurban cars, running and on display. The Niles wooden car #20 was built in 1902. The collection also includes a Jewett car from the CA&E and one from the Chicago, North Shore & Milwaukee line. There are other interurban cars as well.

Other amenities: Gift shop, refreshments, picnic area.

ILLINOIS RAILWAY MUSEUM
P.O. Box 431
Union, IL 60180
(815) 923-2488

Directions: Take I-90 northwest from Chicago, exit at U.S. 20, Marengo, and drive northwest on U.S. 20 to Union.

Open: Daily, June 15 through Labor Day; Saturdays and Sundays, May, June 1 to 15, and the month of September; Sundays only March, April, and November. Cars run from 10:30 A.M. to 5:30 P.M.

Rates: Adults $1.00, two rides for $1.50, children $.50 and $.75.

Features: This is one of the largest and best museums in the country for both trolley and steam road equipment. There are over 125 pieces of rail equipment on display, including numerous streetcars and interurbans. The Chicago area systems are well represented: There are cars from the Chicago, North Shore & Milwaukee, the Chicago, Aurora & Elgin, the Illinois Terminal, and others.

The ride is three miles, over a former railroad line that ran between Elgin and Belvidere, in one of the museum's many trolleys, or possibly in their trolley bus—the only one operating in a transportation museum.

Other amenities: Steam train rides, refreshments, gift shop, picnic area.

INDIANA

INDIANA MUSEUM OF TRANSPORT & COMMUNICATION
P.O. Box 83
Noblesville, IN 46060
(317) 773-0300

Directions: Noblesville is about twenty miles north of Indianapolis. From Indianapolis take State Road 37 north to State Road 32, turn left onto 32, right onto 19. The museum is in Forest Park on State Road 19.

Open: Saturdays, Sundays, and holidays, May through October, 1 P.M. to 6 P.M.

Rates: Adults $1.00, children $.50.

Features: A one-mile round-trip ride in city streetcars or one of their interurban cars. It could be the Chicago, North Shore & Milwaukee coach, or a representative of the Chicago, Aurora & Elgin, the Chicago Transit Authority 4454, or Union Traction of Indiana 429.

Other amenities: Exhibit of paperwork, photographs, and fixtures. A complete trolley research library is maintained at the museum. There are picnic grounds, refreshments, and camping in Forest Park, a gift shop in the museum, a display of horse-drawn vehicles, steam road cars, a hook-and-ladder fire truck and other equipment. There is also a very large operating model layout.

Thomas H. Bader, president of the museum (who signs his letters "Yours trolley," and "Truckingly yours,") says the museum is in "the Interurban Capital [Indianapolis] of the World."

Trolleys

IOWA

MIDWEST OLD SETTLERS AND THRESHERS REUNION
(Not a museum, but close enough to sneak into this list)
Midwest Central Railroad
Box 102
Mt. Pleasant, IA 52641
(319) 385-2912

Directions: Mt. Pleasant is in southeast Iowa, Leave I-90 westbound at Iowa City and take U.S. 218 south to Mt. Pleasant, about fifty miles.

Open: Every year, for five days at the end of August (contact them for the current date), there is a fair that features steam-powered farm equipment, antique cars, and trolleys in the setting of an old Midwest farm village.

Rates: Adults $.75, children $.35.

Features: The Reunion runs open-bench streetcars and interurbans and a steam train. The interurbans are from the Southern Iowa line, and the Waterloo, Cedar Falls & Northern. Others are on display.

Other amenities: Refreshments, gift shop, picnic area, restaurant, trailer parking.

MAINE

SEASHORE TROLLEY MUSEUM
(Run by the New England Electric Railway Historical Society)
P.O. Box 220
Kennebunkport, ME 04046
(207) 967-2712

Directions: From Kennebunk, take Rte 1 north to Log Cabin Road, right on Log Cabin Road to the museum. From Kennebunk*port*, go to the west end of Main Street, north on North Street, which runs into Log Cabin Road. From I-95, use exit 4, go northeast on Rte 111 to Rte 1, right on 1 to Log Cabin Road.

Open: Daily from mid-June to Labor Day weekend; Saturdays, Sundays, Memorial Day, and Columbus Day from the end of May to mid-June, and from early September to Columbus Day. Balance of the year by appointment, with ten days' notice, whenever practicable. 10 A.M. to 6 P.M. on daily schedule, noon to 5 P.M. on weekend schedule.

Rates: Adults $2.00, children $1.00.

Features: During the open season, there are trolley rides every half hour around a looping two-mile track through woods and fields.

Seashore is the oldest and largest trolley museum in the United States, with a collection of more than eighty-five cars, restored, being restored, or waiting to be restored. There is a workshop with a gallery at the museum, so that visitors can see the society's members working to bring the trolley cars back to their original glory.

206

Among Seashore's extensive collection of rolling stock are twelve interurban cars, from the light cars of the New England interurban/suburban railways to the heavy steel interurban car built for the Chicago, Aurora & Elgin (110,000 lbs., 55 tons). It's an excellent place to get an overview of the tremendous variety of interurban and trolley equipment that rolled the rails during the age of the trolley.

Other amenities: Picnic grove, gift shop, displays.

MARYLAND

BALTIMORE STREETCAR MUSEUM
Baltimore Streetcar Museum, Inc.
P.O. Box 7184
Baltimore, MD 21218
(301) 727-9053

Directions: The museum is at the former terminal of the Maryland & Pennsylvania Railroad, at 1901 Falls Road at the northern end of the city.

Open: Sunday afternoons year round, 1 P.M. to 5 P.M.; Thursday evenings during June, July, and August, 7 P.M. to 9 P.M.

Rates: Adults $.50, children $.25.

Features: The museum runs Baltimore streetcars on a one-mile round trip, and has a number of other cars on display, including a horsecar more than a century old and the latest PCC car to operate in Baltimore. No interurbans.

Other amenities: Refreshments, gift shop.

NATIONAL CAPITAL TROLLEY MUSEUM
P.O. Box 5795
Bethesda, MD 20014
(301) 384-9797

Directions: On Bonifant Road between Layhill Road and New Hampshire Avenue, north of Wheaton, Maryland.

Open: Saturdays and Sundays, some holidays, year round, noon to 5 P.M.; June 26 through Labor Day, every day but Monday and Tuesday, noon to 4 P.M.

Rates: Adults $.75, children $.50.

Features: A two-mile ride through the North Branch Regional Park. No interurbans, but some interesting streetcars from Graz, Austria; Dusseldorf; Vienna; and other European cities, as well as from Washington, D.C.

Other amenities: Gift shop, refreshments, operating model railroad, auditorium for film shows, and other events.

MINNESOTA

Minnesota Transportation Museum, Minneapolis
P.O. Box 1300
Hopkins, MN 55343
(612) 729-2428

Directions: At 42nd and Queen Avenue South at Lake Harriet in South Minneapolis.

Open: May 30 through October: Fridays, 6:50 P.M. to dark; Saturdays, 3:30 P.M. to dark; Sundays, 1 P.M. to dark.

Rates: Adults $.30, children $.15.

Features: A small display of trolley cars and a fifteen-minute, one-mile ride over the Como-Harriet line of the Twin City Rapid Transit Co.—a very pretty ride from Lake Harriet to Lake Calhoun through trees and bushes on a private right-of-way. No interurbans.

Other amenities: Picnic area, refreshments nearby.

MISSOURI

National Museum of Transport
3015 Barrett Station Road
St. Louis, MO 63122
(314) 965-6885

Open: Every day but Thanksgiving and Christmas, all year round, 10 A.M. to 5 P.M.

Rates: Adults $2.00, children $.75.

Features: The museum has only stationary displays. Their traction system includes a number of city streetcars and work cars as well as rail transit vehicles such as subway cars and "el" equipment.

In interurban stock, they display three different types of car from the Illinois Terminal Railroad: #104, a heavy (58,000 lbs.) suburban center-door electric car; #241 (83,000 lbs.), a classic interurban with arched stained glass windows; and #410, a lightweight (42,000 lbs.), which saw service until 1958.

Other amenities: Refreshments, gift shop.

OHIO

Trolleyville, U.S.A.
7100 B Columbia Road
Olmsted Falls, OH 44138
(216) 235-4725

Directions: The museum is at the Columbia Park Shopping Center on Rte 252, a short distance southwest of Cleveland.

Open: Sundays and holidays from Memorial Day to the end of September, 1 P.M. to 6 P.M.

Rates: Adults $.75, children $.50.

Features: Unlike other operating trolley museums, the great majority of which are run by a group of railfan volunteers, Trolleyville is the project of longtime railfan Gerald Brookings, who owns the shopping center in which it is located. He has found the streetcars and interurbans that run at Trolleyville or are on display there and commissioned their restoration. (And what a beautiful job has been done!)

You'll be able to ride the two-and-a-half-mile trip in an open-bench trolley from Vera Cruz, Mexico; in light and heavy interurbans from the Chicago, Aurora & Elgin; or in cars from the Shaker Rapid.

Other amenities: Displays, gift shop.

OHIO RAILWAY MUSEUM
P.O. Box 171
Worthington, OH 43085
(614) 885-7345

Directions: The museum is in the Columbus metropolitan area, just off Ohio Rte 161, one mile west of I-71. From I-71, take exit 61.

Open: Saturdays, Sundays, and holidays, June through August; Sundays only, April, May, September, October, and November; 1 P.M. to 5 P.M. Saturdays, 12:30 P.M. to 5:30 P.M. Sundays, 1 P.M. to 4:30 P.M. in April, 1 P.M. to 5 P.M. in November.

Rates: Nominal fares according to their brochure.

Features: There are one-and-a-half miles of track (a three-mile round trip) through woods and fields. The steam train runs every third weekend in the summer on the same track.

The museum owns streetcars and interurbans, and steam road equipment. They started with Ohio Public Service Interurban #21, which is the best example we have of wooden interurban car design—the Niles Combine—and still a functional, well-preserved beauty. You will also find here an Illinois Terminal PCC interurban, a Cincinnati & Lake Erie interurban, and a Chicago, North Shore & Milwaukee line car.

Other amenities: An operating railway signal system, a full-size reproduction of a small-town depot of the 1890s, and an exhibit of railroadiana. Also a gift shop.

OREGON

TROLLEY PARK
(Run by the Oregon Electric Railway Historical Society)
Star Route, Box 1318
Glenwood, OR 97120
(503) 357-3574

Directions: Go northwest from Portland on Canyon Road (which is Sunset Highway

Trolleys

and U.S. Rte 26). Turn left onto Oregon Rte 6 at Tillamook Junction, go through the communities of Banks and Glenwood, and follow Park signs.

Open: Weekends and holidays, Memorial Day to July 4 and Labor Day to October. From July 4 to Labor Day, open daily (except Monday), 11 A.M. to sunset.

Rates: Adults $1.00, children $.50, families $2.50.

Features: Unless you are an overnight camper (and you can be), you must ride the trolleys from the public road to the twenty-six-acre camping and picnic grounds at the far end of the valley, past the shops and railway work area into the forest.

You may find yourself doing this on a double-decker from Blackpool, England, on an Australian open bench, or the museum's interurban, #1304 from British Columbia Electric Railway.

Other amenities: Gift shop with some picnic supplies, overnight camping, fishing, swimming, trolley displays.

PENNSYLVANIA

Buckingham Valley Trolley Association, Buckingham Valley
3001 Robin Lane
Havertown, PA 19083
No phone. For possible help call New Hope & Ivyland Railroad (215) 862-5206.

Directions: Cars leave from the terminal of the New Hope & Ivyland steam road and ride over part of their track. The terminal is on Rte 413, just south of Rte 263 in Buckingham. Buckingham is in Bucks County, just north of Philadelphia and southwest of New Hope.

Open: Saturdays and Sundays, June through November. Frequent trips during the day.

Features: Rides are operating now, on the NH & I tracks, for a one-mile trip. In the planning stage at this writing is a more extensive project that will include a museum. The BVTA has acquired the cars of the former Trolley Valhalla in New Jersey and plans to set them up in a museum in its Pennsylvania location. Operating now is the double-truck 1918 trolley from the Red Arrow Line in Pennsylvania.

Other amenities: Gift shop, picnic grounds.

Railways to Yesterday, Orbisonia
328 North 28th Street
Allentown, PA 18104
(814) 447-9576 (weekends only)

Directions: The trolley ride and museum at the East Broad Top (steam) Railroad, Rockhill Furnace, Huntingdon County, Pa., are on Rte 522, north of the Pennsylvania Turnpike exits 13 and 14, above Shade Gap, Pa. This area is almost exactly between Pittsburgh and Philadelphia, in the center of the state and southeast of Altoona. The trolley museum is directly across the street from the Orbisonia station of the East Broad Top narrow gauge steam railway.

Open: Weekends and holidays, Memorial Day through October; and for the Winter Spectacular, mid-February, noon to 5 P.M.

Rates: Adults $.75, children $.35.

Features: A one-mile line on which the Shade Gap Electric Railway operates a two-mile round trip in its large open-bench streetcar, and occasionally in #315, a Chicago, Aurora & Elgin Railroad composite interurban coach built in 1909.
The railway owns twenty trolleys; #315 is a favorite with the members, according to G. Wayne Leopple of the museum, and they particularly enjoy it during their annual Winter Spectacular—it has heat!
At the Spectacular, or if it should snow before the end of October, visitors may see the snow sweeper, built in 1910 for the Chicago & Joliet Electric, later seeing service in Scranton, Pa. The museum still uses it occasionally to clear snow from the tracks.

Other amenities: The narrow-gauge steam road, which uses a five-mile section of track that was part of the original working route of the road. Refreshments, gift shop, picnic area. The Swigart Auto Museum and the Lincoln and Indian Caverns are nearby. A very good place to visit!

ARDEN TROLLEY MUSEUM, Washington, Pa.
(Run by the Pennsylvania Railway Museum Association)
Pennsylvania Railway Museum Association
P.O. Box 832
Pittsburgh, PA 15230
(412) 222-9986

Directions: Washington is just west and south of Pittsburgh. The museum is about two miles from downtown Washington, on North Main Street extension.

Open: Saturdays, Sundays, and holidays, May through October, 1 P.M. to 6 P.M.

Rates: Adults $.50, children $.25.

Features: Pittsburgh trolley cars are on display, as well as some from New Orleans and Philadelphia. An interurban car from the former Pittsburgh Railways line to Washington, Pa., runs on a mile of its former working route.

Other amenities: Refreshments, gift shop, picnic grounds. In the nearby South Side of Pittsburgh, you can ride the incline—the inclined trolleys that afford a panorama of Pittsburgh's rivers, bridges, and hills while taking your breath away with the steepness of their track.

WASHINGTON

PUGET SOUND AND SNOQUALMIE VALLEY RAILROAD, Snoqualmie
(Run by the Puget Sound Railway Historical Association)
Puget Sound Railway Historical Association
Box 3801
Seattle, WA 98124
(206) 888-0373

Directions: Take I-90 to Snoqualmie Falls exit, go left at first light. From Seattle the #210 Issaquah/North Bend bus will take you to the museum.

Open: Saturdays, Sundays, and holidays, July and August; Sundays, April through June, and September and October; 11 A.M. to 5 P.M..

Rates: Adults $1.00, children $.50, families $2.50, senior citizens $.50. (Note: The one-and-a-half-mile round trip is being lengthened; when it is, the fare will go up.)

Features: The museum is devoted principally to steam road equipment, but it does have some trolley cars. There is a thirty-minute guided tour of the equipment on display.

Other amenities: Refreshments, gift shop, picnic grounds.

YAKIMA INTERURBAN TROLLEY LINES
P.O. Box 124
Yakima, WA 98907
(509) 452-5211

Directions: Board the trolley at the Whitney School, 44th Avenue and Nob Hill Boulevard, Yakima, or call the twenty-four-hour answering service (452-5211) to verify time and place.

Open: Trolleys run Saturdays, 9 A.M. to 12 noon; Sundays, 12 noon to 5 P.M., year round. Schedules, though frequent, are not regular, and you should write or call before planning a trip.

Features: Something rather special—not a museum, but an operating interuban line of some twenty-odd miles. The rides are a Bicentennial project of Yakima and Yakima County. There are several different routes, covering different sections of the track, and the rides last about half an hour.

The cars were found in Portugal, after a long search for the trolleys that had traveled this line when it was an operating interurban railway. They have been restored and painted, and are now proudly running through the fruit orchards and communities near Yakima. They are available for charter.

ONTARIO (CANADA)

HALSTON COUNTY RADIAL RAILWAY, Rockwood
(Run by the Ontario Electric Railway Historical Association)
Ontario Electric Railway Historical Association
Box 121
Scarborough, Ontario, Canada MIK 5B9

Directions: The museum is between Cambellsville Road and Fourth Line, just south of Rockwood, Ontario, eight miles north of exit 38 of Highway 401. Rockwood is near Toronto and to the northwest of that city.

Open: Saturdays, Sundays, and holidays, from the end of May to the end of October, 11 A.M. to 5 P.M. (Remember, a holiday in the U.S. may not be a holiday in Canada. Check first.)

Rates: Nominal fares, according to their letter.

Features: "Radial" is the word used in some parts of Canada to describe an interurban railway. This museum's brochure points out that it is "a museum with a difference . . . not a building full of static exhibits in mothballs, but . . . an operating railway you can see and ride." It has a mile of track, and on it you may find any one of its operating cars. It may be the London & Port Stanley #8, a Canadian interurban, or possibly the Montreal & Southern Counties Railway #107, which is nearing the end of the restoration work on it as this is being written.

There is a great deal of electric railway equipment on display, including several work cars: a line car, a crane car, a sweeper, and the components of an electric freight train.

QUEBEC (CANADA)

CANADIAN RAILWAY MUSEUM
(Run by the Canadian Railway Historical Association)
P.O. Box C.P. 148
St. Constant, Quebec, Canada
(514) 632-2410

Directions: From downtown Montreal, cross the Mercier Bridge and go east along Rte 9C. Turn left at the second stoplight. Or follow Rte 3 south toward the U.S. border, take exit marked "Rte 9C, Mercier Bridge," and turn left at second stoplight. From the U.S. border, follow Rte 9 toward Montreal, exit at "9C, Mercier Bridge," etc. The museum entrance is at 122A St.-Pierre Street in St. Constant, which is ten miles from downtown Montreal and about thirty miles from the U.S. border.

Open: Daily from the second week in May until Labor Day, and weekends from Labor Day to the end of October, 10 A.M. to 17 hrs. (5 P.M.).

Rates: Adults $1.50, children $.75. Rides on train or streetcar, one for $.15, two for $.25.

Features: There is a static display of over a hundred steam, electric, and Diesel locomotives, other steam road equipment, streetcars and interurbans—a graphic history of Canada's railways. The rides are irregular; check if it's important to catch one, although there is a great deal to see in the excellent displays here.

Other amenities: Refreshments, gift shop, picnic area.

Index

Ackerman, Martin, 42, 75, 79
ACT-1 (Advanced Concept Train), 194
Air brakes, 98
Air Force Museum, 149
Air Line News, The, 59, 61
Air Line Park, 62
Akron, Ohio, 40, 41, 69, 104
Akron, Bedford & Cleveland Line, 9,
   41, 42, 48, 72, 82
Alko Line, 99
Alliance, Ohio, 41
Alpine Division, 94
"American Ground Transport" (Snell),
   101–102
Amusement parks, trips to, 57–58
Anti-climber (device), 67–68
Arden Trolley Museum, 211
Arrowhead Springs, Calif., 93
Ashtabula, Ohio, 79
Atlanta, Ga., 41, 42, 175, 176, 177–180
Atlantic Richfield Oil Company, 192
Automatic signaling, 67

Back-of-the-car men (conductors), 77–
   78
Bader, Thomas, 160

*Badger Traction: The Story of the
   Smaller Electric Railways of
   Wisconsin* (Central Electric
   Railfans Association), 112
Balboa, Calif. 93
Baltimore Streetcar Museum, 207
Bay Area Electric Railroad Association,
   186–188
Bay Area Rapid Transit (BART), 122–
   123, 193, 196
Bedford, Ohio, 41
Bell, Joe, 176, 177
Berman, Arnold, 113–116
Bicknell, Warren, 64–65
Block signaling, 67
Bloomington, Ill., 85
Bob's Custom Finishers, 108–109
Boeing Vertol cars, 103
Boeing Vertol Corporation, 122, 193
Boeing Vertol Light Rail Vehicle, 194
Bonner Railwagon, 42
Borrup, Roger, 113
Bowers, Dana K., 165–166
Box motors, 29–32, 38
Boxcars, 18, 91
Brake systems, 27, 98

Branford Electric Railway Association, 165
Branford Trolley Museum, 128, 167–185, 193, 203
Pageant of Trolleys, 180–181
Brewster, N. Y., 197
Broadway Limited, 121
Brookings, Gerald, 190
Brotherhood of Railroad Trainmen, 139
Buckingham Valley Trolley Association, 210
Buffalo, N. Y., 14, 52
Businger, James, 25–27, 37, 44, 113, 197

Cable cars, 4, 193
Caldwell, Bernard, 109–110, 113, 116
California Railway Museum, 202
Camden, N. J., 193
Camden County, Maine, 37
Canadian Railway Museum, 213
Canfield, Joseph, 113
Canton, Ohio, 48
Carillon Park, 149
Carlinville, Ill., 85
Carlisle and Finch Company, 125
Carson, O. E., 174–181, 182
Carstens, Hal, 122
Cass family, 42–43
Cedar Point, Ohio, 52
Central Electric Railfans Association, 112, 121
Central Electric Railway Association, 8
Central Pacific Railroad, 93
Central States Electric Line, 130, 131, 132, 135
Chagrin Falls, Ohio, 10
Champaign, Ill., 85
Chesapeake & Ohio Railroad, 157, 165
Chicago, 14, 42, 49, 165
Chicago, Aurora and Elgin Line, 32
Chicago, Burlington & Quincy Railroad, 59

Chicago–New York Electric Air Line Railroad, 59–62
construction of, 62
investors in, 59–60
proposal for, 59–60
Chicago, Ottawa & Peoria Line, 88
Chicago, South Shore & South Bend (C,SS&SB), 165
Chicago & Eastern Illinois, 91
Chicago Transit System, 121
Chicago and Wheaton Electric Railway, 21
Chico, Calif., 14
Chittenden, Rea F., 87
Cincinnati, Ohio, 11, 49, 103
Cincinnati cars, 28
Cinncinatti & Lake Erie, 42, 103
City trolly cars, 3–6, 7–8
Cleveland, Ohio, 9–10, 11, 34, 39, 41, 42, 46, 49, 52, 64–66
Cleveland, Painesville & Ashtabula, 64, 68, 75, 77
Cleveland, Southwestern & Columbus Railway, 15, 35–36, 79, 135–136, 137
Cleveland, Southwestern Line, 23, 25, 48, 68, 81, 105
Cleveland & Eastern Traction Company, 9–10, 19, 52
Cleveland Heights, Ohio, 10
Cleveland *Plain Dealer*, 40
Cleveland "Rapid," 75
Cleveland Transit System, 72
Clinton, Ill., 85
Coke Region system, 99
Colorado Railroad Museum, 203
Columbus, Ohio, 44, 103
"Combination" car, 35
Commonwealth & Southern, 104
Connecticut Electric Railway Association, 188
Connecticut Electric Railway Museum, 27

Connecticut Valley chapter (National
  Railway Historical Society), 112
Connellsville, Pa., 99
Convention and Visitors' Bureau of the
  city of Yakima, 185
Conway, Thomas, 103, 196
Cooperstown, N.Y., 140
Cope, David, 135
Corona, Calif., 93
Cox, Harold, 113
"Creep" doors, 37
Crestline, Ohio, 14
Crew and trainmen, 75–83
  dispatchers, 65–67
  holdups, 76–77
  occupational hazards, 78–79
  pay scale, 77
  suspensions, 78
  weather conditions and, 79–83
Crime, 76–77
Cummings, O. R., 113

Danville, Ill., 85
Darst, Harry, 135
Dayton, Ohio, 103, 193
Decatur, Ill., 85
Delta Queen, 181
Derr, John, 135
Des Moines & Central Iowa Interurban
  Railway, 38–39
Detroit, Mich., 11, 39, 40, 49, 52
Dial-a-Ride buses, 193
Diaz, Joe, 113
Dispatcher, role of, 65–67, 77
Dolores, 35–36
Dosey, Herbert, 22, 23, 25, 32, 41, 135–
  137, 197
Due, John F., x, 112
Dynamic braking (gooseneck hand
  brake), 98

*Easy-to-Build Model Railroad Struc-
  tures*, 113

Edison, Thomas, 6
*Electric Interurban Railways in
  America, The* (Hilton and Due),
  x
Electric Package Company, 42
"Electric Parks," 53
Electric Railroaders' Association, 96,
  107, 117–124, 181
  convention program, 121
  founded, 118, 124
  "juice jack" enthusiasts, 118
  membership, 118
Electric Railway Dictionary, The, 112
Electric Railway Journal, The, 9, 113
Electric Railways of Northeastern Ohio
  (Central Electric Railfans
  Association), 112
Electrical Installation Company of
  Chicago, 10–11
Electroliners, 85, 91
Elkhart Lake, Wis., 14
Els, 123
Elyria, Ohio, 105
Erkfitz, Harry, 135
Euclid Beach Amusement Park, 58
Everett, Henry A., 34
Everett, Moore, Pomeroy, Mandel-
  baum, and Appleyard, 9, 23,
  34, 48
Extra cars, 47, 77

Fairfield Models Company, 114
Fitch, Lyle C., 101
Fitchburg, Mass., 55
Fleming, J. N., 47
Ford, Henry, 10
Ford Motor Company, 10, 40
Fort Wayne, Ind., 14, 37–38
Foulds, Blair, 37, 128–135, 137–138,
  147, 153, 160
Franchises, 17, 104
Frederick, Homer, 72

Freight operations, 38–43, 89–91, 93, 99,
    104, 165
  local, 40–41
  long-distance, 41–42
  piggyback, 42
Front-of-the-car men (motormen), 77–
    78
Funerals, 34–36
Gary, Ind., 49, 62, 165
Gates Mills, Ohio, 10, 19, 47, 52
Gauge, track, 23, 95
Geauga County, Ohio, 10
General Motors Corporation, 100–103
  Dieselization program of, 101–103
George, Leon, 41, 82
Georgia Power Company, 180
Glendale, Calif., 93
Glendale-Burbank Line, 94
Glenwood, Gregg, 157
Glenwood, Oregon, 185
Gordon, W. R., 113
Goshen, Ind., 11
Grain elevators, 91
Grand Central Terminal, 96, 197
Great Epizootic of 1872, 4, 101
Great Lakes Naval Training Station, 49
Great Northern Railroad, 117, 120
Gregg, Newton, 112

Hagerstown & Frederick Line, 95
Halston County Radial Railway
    Museum, 167, 212–213
Harlem Division (New York Central
    Railroad), 197
Harmony, Pa., 41
Hartwick, N.Y., 142
Hazards and accidents, 63–75
  from animals, 73–74
  bizarre type of, 72–73
  car weight factor in, 69–71
  through carelessness, 68–69
  crew members and, 75–83
  dispatchers and, 65–67

  head-on collisions, 68
  heroism, 74–75
  holdup, 76–77
  safety device precautions, 67–68
  "split switch," 69
  weather condtions and, 79–83
Headlights, 27
Headlights, 118
Heinemann, William, 38–39, 49, 79
Heinz, H. J., 10–11
Hibernia, Ohio, 76
Hilton, George W., x, 112
Ho Primer, 113
HO scale, 123, 134, 135, 143, 151–152,
    164
Holland, Harris P., 85
Holland Palace Car Company, 85
Hollywood, Calif., 94
Hoover, Amelia J., 21
Hoover Vacuum Cleaner Company, 48
Hord, U. P., 60–61
Horn, George, 122
Horsecars, 3–4
Huntington, Collis P., 93
Huntington, Henry E., 34, 92, 93, 94, 95

Illinois Railway Museum, 204–205
Illinois Terminal Railroad (ITR), 22, 84–
    91, 92, 131
  end of, 91
  equipment, 85, 90–91
  freight business, 89–91
  passenger decline, 91
  sleeper car service, 85–86
  trackage, 85
Illinois Traction Company, 22, 84
Indiana Electric Railway, 155
Indiana Museum of Transport and
    Communication, 159–160, 188,
    205
Indiana Railroad, 37
Indianapolis, Ind., 11, 14
Indianapolis & Southern Railway, 175

Indianapolis Traction Terminal, 8
Institute of Public Administration, 101
Interborough Rapid Transit (IRT
  subway line), 14
International Railway, 52
Interstate Commerce Commission
  (ICC), 102
Interurban Interlude (Quinby), 182
Interurban railways:
  beginning of, 3–15
  design and color, 23–25
  differences between, 16–46
  end of, 100–106
  first electric, 3
  future role of, 192–198
  hazards and accidents, 63–75
  as a hobby, 107–164
  introduction to, ix–xi
  largest trackage, 8
  last cars built, 85
  longest continuous trip, 14
  most grandiose scheme for, 56–62
  museums, 165–191, 201–213
  only line still operating (1970s), 165
  special function cars, 32–43
  trips and journeys, 44–58
  See also names of lines

Jackson, Mich., 14
Johnson, James D., 113
Johnson, Tom L., 48
Jones, Vane, 113
Josephine, 34
  race from Toledo to Cleveland (1910),
  65
Judiciary Committee (U.S. Senate), 101

Kalmbach, Al, 122
Kalmbach and Carstens 112, 113
Kalmbach and Company, 155
Kane, John, 110
Kanell, Samuel, 193
Kansas City, Mo., 14

Kennebunkport, Maine, 27
Kennywood Park, 53–54
Kingsland, Ind., 68
Kit bashing, 108, 131, 142
Knox County Electric Railway, 37
Korea, 175
Krambles, George, 121
Kulp, Randolph, 113

Lajoie, William, 69
Lake Erie and Southern Line, 137
Lake Shore Electric Pioneers
  Association, 75
Lake Shore Electric Railway, 32, 39–40,
  42, 45, 52, 60, 63–65, 73, 74, 79,
  100, 104, 105, 146
Lang, William, 74–75
Laport, Ind., 62
Leflin, Addison, Jr., 187–188
Lehigh Valley Railroad, 129
Lehigh Valley Transit Company, 8
Light Rail Vehicles (LRVs), 122, 194
Limited, The, 63–64
Lindenwold, N.J., 193
Lindenwold Line, 193
Lionel Company, 125
Long, Bryant, 38
Lorain, Ohio, 48–49
Los Angeles, Calif., 14, 38, 93, 94
Los Angeles Interurban Railway, 93
Los Angeles Metropolitan Coach Lines,
  94
Louisville, Ky., 11, 14
Louisville & Nashville, 42
Lundin, Oscar A., 100

McGraw, Harrison B., 19
Mackinaw, Ill., 85
McKinley, William B., 88
Madison, Ga., 176, 177
Mail by Rail (Long), 38
Mansfield, Ohio, 48
Marvin, Clarence, 69

Marx, Samuel, 49
Mayer, Louis B., 49–52
*Mayer & Thalberg, The Make-Believe
    Saints* (Marx), 49
Mellon, Andrew, 54
Meriden (Connecticut) Electric Railway,
    69
Metro-Goldwyn-Mayer (MGM), 49
Meyers, F. J., 48
Meyers Pump Company, 48
Middleton, William, 113
Midwest Old Settlers and Threshers
    Reunion, 206
Miller, Alexander C., 59, 60, 61, 68
Minnesota Transportation Museum, 208
Model Railroad Magazine, 155
Model Railroader, 112, 122, 134
Model railroading, 107–164
    devotion of enthusiasts to, 107–116
    ERA and, 107. 117–124
    kit bashing, 108, 131, 142
    number of enthusiasts, 108
    popularity of, 125
    prizes for construction, 161–164
    prototypes, 148
    "Rails Alive '75" Convention, 146–
        164
    scale accuracy, 125–145
Model Railway Industry Association
    (MRIA), 155
Monongahela Street Railways, 54
Monoroad, The, 109
Monroeville, Ohio, 65
Montreal sightseeing car, 27
Mora, Jeffrey, J. G., 196
Moran, Iowa, 38–39
Moulton, J. S., 14
Mount Lowe Line, 94
Mount Lowe Springs, 94
MU (multiple unit control), 6
Mumford, Lewis, ix–x
Museums, 165–191
    administrative tasks, 189–190

list of, 201–213
meaning of, 165
number of, 107
trolley restoration projects, 169–174
types of visitors to, 190–191
volunteer workers, 188
See also names of museums

N scale, 125
National Capital Trolley Museum, 207
National Model Railroad Association
    (NMRA), 134, 146–164
    Certificate of Conformance, 146–147
    Dayton, Ohio, convention ("Rails
        Alive '75"), 146–164
    formed, 146
    Gold Lantern Award, 161, 163
    prize-winning models, 161–164
National Museum of Transport, 208
National Railway Historical Society,
    112
New Castle, Ind., 37–38
New Haven Railroad, 102
New Orleans, La., 193
New York, Westchester & Boston, 111–
    114
New York Central Railroad, 14, 59, 60,
    70, 110, 117, 140, 197
New York City Transit Authority, 109
Newark, N.J., 193
Niagara Falls, N.Y., 52
Nickel Plate Railroad, 42
Nonelectric rear lights, 67
Northern Ohio Power & Light, 104
Northern Ohio Traction & Light
    Company (NOTL), 9, 23, 48, 66,
    69, 104

O scale, 125, 135, 159–160
Oakland, Calif., 42
Oberlin College, 44, 73
Ohio Central Traction Company, 14–15
Ohio Railway Museum, 209

Ohio State University, 44
Ohmer registers, 77
Oil lamps, 29
Old Johnson 3-fare line, 48–49
Olmsted Falls, Ohio, 190
Oneonta, N.Y., 14, 139, 142
Orange Empire Trolley Museum, 201–
    202
Oregon Electric Railway Historical
    Society, 185
Orr, Dick, 151–153

Pacific Electric Railway, 34, 38, 49–52,
    84, 92–94
    distances covered, 93
    end of, 94
    excursion rides, 94
    freight operations, 93
    types of cars used, 93–94
    World War II, 94
Palliser's Model Homes 1876, 157
Panic of 1903, 48
Panic of 1907, 48
Parcel Dispatch service, 46
Penn Central Railroad, 102
Pennsylvania Railroad, 3, 10, 14–15, 60
Pennsylvania Trolley gauge, 95
Peoria, Ill., 85
Peru, Ind., 11
Peters, Charles, 46, 69, 77, 81
Philadelphia, Pa., 193, 194
Piggyback freight hauling, 42
Pittsburgh, Pa., 14, 41, 49, 53–54, 95,
    99, 193
Pittsburgh Pickle Company, 10
Platt, Ward, 45–46, 52, 70, 75, 77
Pomeroy and Mandelbaum, 23
Port Authority Transit (PATCO), 193
Portman, Warren, 108–112, 113
Post office lines, 37–38
Presidents' Conference Car (PCC), 103
Presidents' Conference Car of 1933, 196
Price, Jonathan D., 60, 61

Private cars, 32–34
Prototype trips, 148
Puget Sound Railway Historical
    Association Museum, 211–212
Putnam Division Line (New York
    Central), 140

Quinby, E. J., 107, 118, 124, 181–182

Radial couplers, 90–91
Radial railways. *See* Interurban
    railways
Rail Technology Division (Department
    of Transportation), 194–196
Railettes, 149, 161
Railroad, 111
Railway Model Craftsman, 122
Railways to Yesterday (museum), 210–
    211
Ravenna, Ohio, 69
"Red Devils," 103
Redlands, Calif., 93
R.E.L.I.C. Trolley Museum, 204
Rice, Alan L., 113
Richfield Springs, N.Y., 140, 142
Richmond, Va., 6
Rights-of-way, 16–21, 46, 91
Rinke, Herman, 96, 107, 117, 119–120,
    122, 181
Rio Vista Junction, Calif., 187
Riverside, Calif., 49–52, 93
Robinson, Peck, 65
Robinson circus, 38–39
Rochester, N.Y., 14, 193
Rockland County, Maine, 37
Roof mat protection, 28–29
Roosevelt, Theodore, 75
Rotary converter equipment, 8
Roundhouse I, II, and III, 109

Sacramento, Calif., 14, 187
Sacramento Northern Railway, 135, 186
Safety devices, 67–68

Safety fender, 74
St. Joseph, Mo., 14
St. Louis, Mo., 85, 86, 87–89
St. Louis and Florissant Line, 37
San Bernardino, Calif., 14, 38, 49–52, 93
San Fernando, Calif., 93
San Francisco, Calif., 14, 42, 94, 122–123, 187, 196
Sandusky, Ohio, 52, 70
Santa Ana, Calif., 49–52, 93
Sas, Bert, 114
Schlegel, Frank, 104, 128, 131, 132, 134–135, 140, 144, 146
Schlegel, Mrs. Frank, 168–169
School trains, 36
Seashore Trolley Museum, 27, 107, 182, 206–207
Seattle World's Fair, 196
Seville, Ohio, 48
Seyfried, VIncent, 113
Shaker Heights, Ohio, 49, 175, 193
Shaker Rapid Transit, 49, 175
Sheldon, John, 138–145
Sheldon, Mrs. John, 143
Sieberling, Kelly, 46
Silien, Joseph S., 194
Silver Lake Junction, Ohio, 41
Sleepers, 34, 85–86
Sleet cutter, 82
Sleet on trolley wire, 82–83
Smith, Leila, 74–75
Smoking cars, 21, 35, 45
Snell, Bradford, 101–102
Snow, Ernest, 132, 135
Solano County, Calif., 187
Somers, Richard, 133
South Bend, Ind., 14, 49
Southern New York Railway, 139–140
Southern Pacific Railroad, 93
Spittoons, 34
Split switch accidents, 69
Spock, Benjamin, 10

Spokane and Moscow Line, 38
Sprague, Frank Julian, 6, 8
Sprague Library, 124
Springfield, Ill., 85, 86
"State of the Art" car (SOAC), 194
Stops, 16–17
  frequency of, 63, 64
Streator, Ill., 88
Street Railway Journal, 113, 180
Street trolleys, beginning of, 4–6
Studebaker, J. M., 10–11
Subcommittee on Antitrust and Monopoly (U.S. Senate), 101
Summer property, traveling to, 47
Sunday, Billy, 10–11
Sussman, Charley, 146
Sweetman, Joe, 182
Syracuse, N.Y., 14

Takaido Express, 121
Tappan Zee Model Railroad Club, 134, 141
Temporary Land Bank, 193
Thalberg, Irving, 49–52
Third-rail electrification, 8
Tickets, buying, 16
Tiffin, Ohio, 9
Toilets, 22–23, 27
Toledo, Ohio, 11, 42, 52, 64–66
Town franchises, 17
Track Standards Committee, 153
Traction Guidebook, 138, 140
Traction Heritage, 113
Traction and Models, 113
Traction orange, 25
"Traction Plans Index" (Foulds), 147
Traction Standards Committee (National Model Railroad Association), 147
Train Shed Cyclopedia, 112
Trains, 122
Transport of New Jersey, 193
Transportation, 112

Travel Town Museum, 201
Trips and journeys, 44–58
    to amusement parks, 53–58
    of city residents (to the countryside), 47
    commuter, 45–46
    to excursion spots, 52–53
    of farmers' wives (to the city), 46
    labor market and, 47–49
    local errands, 44–45
    for sneak movie previews, 49–52
    sports activities, 44, 49
    Sunday courtship, 54–55
Trolley, meaning of, 6
Trolley flash, 78
Trolley League baseball teams, 49
Trolley Park (Oregon), 185–186, 209–210
Trolley Talk (Wagner), 113
"Trolleys, by Gollys" (Bicentennial project), 185
Trolleyville, U.S.A., 190, 208–209
Truss rods, 29

Uniontown, Pa., 99
U.S. Department of Transportation, 194–196
United States Steel Corporation, 48, 62
United Transportation Union, 161
Utah-Idaho Central Railroad, 36

Van Sweringen brothers, 49
Venice, Ill., 86–87
Vermillion, Ohio, 45–46
Vermillion Marine Museum, 136

Wachinsky, John, 146
Wagner, Birdella, 113
Wagner, Richard, 113
Warehouse Point, Conn., 27
Warehouse Point Trolley Museum, 203–204
Warsaw, Ind., 11
Waterloo, Cedar Falls & Northern Railroad, 42–43
West Penn Railways, 84, 95–99
    air brake devices, 98
    "Coke Region" system, 99
    end of, 99
    freight operations, 99
    track gauge and signaling, 95–98
Westinghouse electromagnetic track brake, 98
Wheelbarrow suspension, system of, 6
Whistles, 27, 69
Wilcox, Ed., 36, 41, 73, 75–76, 81
Wilcox, Max, 35–36, 105
Winona Assembly, 10–11
Winona Interurban, 11
Winona Lakes, Ind., 11
Wissinger, John, 159
World War I, 49, 101
World War II, 94
Wright brothers, 147

Yakima, Wash., 185
Yakima Valley Interurban Lines, 185, 212
Yakima Valley Transportation Company, 185
Youngstown, Ohio, 14, 41